For
Marian - If you
enjoyed it the first
time hope you'll enjoy
it now.

[signature]
USMC (ret)
Feb 7, 1999

# The Cardinal in the Chancery and Other Recollections

# The Cardinal in the Chancery and Other Recollections

## Alfred Puhan
### U.S. Ambassador (Ret.)

**VANTAGE PRESS**
New York ● Los Angeles

FIRST EDITION

Copyright © 1990 by Alfred Puhan, U.S. Ambassador (Ret.)

Published by Vantage Press, Inc.
516 West 34th Street, New York, New York 10001

Manufactured in the United States of America
ISBN: 0-533-08843-7

Library of Congress Catalog Card No.: 89-90519

To Mandy, Travis, Kevin, Courtney, Shevonne, Lexie, Evan, and last, but no means least, Jeanne

# Contents

# *Preface*

I began writing this little book as a legacy for my three children and their children. It is an account of a long life spent in interesting places at interesting times: London during the war years, debating with Joseph Goebbels over the air waves; Vienna and the making of the Austrian Treaty, which gave Austria its freedom; Bangkok, at the beginning of the build-up for Vietnam; Washington during some crucial years in our relations with NATO and Germany; Budapest and the liberation of Cardinal Mindszenty after his fifteen years in the American Embassy. I participated in these events—sometimes as a bit player, others as a principal. Most of these memoirs were written from memory, and no doubt contain some errors. These memories are all mine. Some of the best suggestions came from my wife, Jeanne, who also performed the onerous task of typing and retyping the manuscript.

# The Cardinal in the Chancery and Other Recollections

# Author's Note

This book was written before the momentous changes in the face of Europe. If my chapters on Germany and Hungary have been overtaken by these events, it should be remembered that scarcely anyone in 1988 and 1989 expected the Berlin Wall to crumble so quickly, or that Hungary would be allowed to have free democratic elections in 1990. I plead guilty, along with most experts, to a lack of prescience when I wrote these words.

# Beginnings

THE Vistula River forms a delta just before it empties its waters into the Bay of Danzig (Gdansk) and the Baltic Sea. From its source to its several mouths is a distance of nearly seven hundred miles. Along its shores lie ancient Polish and German cities. Through the centuries, invading armies have traversed its waters: the Lithuanians, the Poles, the Teutonic knights, Swedes, the Prussians, the Russians, the Germans, the armies of Napoleon and Hitler, and finally, the Russians again.

It was along the shores of the North and Baltic seas that my forebears traveled to settle in the border region of Prussia and Russia. From a distant relative (a dignified man in his sixties, who worked in the treasury of the West German government in Bonn) I learned that the name we shared originated in the Netherlands—the spelling perhaps somewhat different from what it is today. I heard my father speak of Bromberg, Deutsch-Eylau, Marienwerder, and Preussisch Holland.

The Puhans became farmers, one branch of the family settling in the area around Lodz in Poland. What became of them my relative in Bonn did not know. Another branch of the family stayed in the Prusso-Russo borderlands.

My paternal grandfather, Ernst Puhan, a man with a typical nineteenth century beard, had four sons and (although I am not entirely certain of this) one daughter. Some time in the last half of the nineteenth century, he took his family to the U.S.A., then known as the land of milk and honey, to seek fame and fortune, which had eluded him in his native land. He apparently moved across the U.S. as the pioneers did, going westward. Although my father was most reticent talking about his family, I did learn from him that the family probably got as far west as Kansas City, Missouri. Precisely what my grandfather did in this country, I was never able to learn. He apparently made a living and was able to support his family. From all the evidence I have been able to gather, he died in the U.S., probably as a U.S. citizen, although citizenship was not at that time as clearly defined as it is today. His death occurred in the first decade of the twentieth century. He left an aging wife, four sons, and possibly one daughter.

The oldest son, and probably the most interesting of the family, was Emil. He had received a good education in Germany, had attended the Gymnasium, and was able to write fluently in Latin and Greek. A classical education was not uncommon in those days. Interestingly enough, he never pursued a trade, but became a hobo. He wandered around the world from one country to another, apparently having little difficulty crossing borders, and on occasion would visit his more affluent brother Oscar.

This was always a source of embarrassment to Uncle Oscar, since Emil was regarded as the black sheep of the family. Oscar, the second son, purchased land on North Clark Street in Chicago, on which he built a garage. The land, which later became part of the Loop, appreciated in value and became phenomenally expensive. He was able, at the age of thirty-five, to retire as a gentleman farmer in a small Illinois town called Sandwich, some sixty-five miles south and west of Chicago.

Oscar married an attractive woman, Aunt Susie, whom I remember quite well. When I knew her, she had become rather corpulent, but there were still traces of her once great beauty. They had no children. They bought what I thought at the time was a rather large house in a wooded section on the outskirts of Sandwich. (I realized later that it was quite small). Sandwich was a town of less than two thousand people. Here Oscar settled down with his wife, to the life of a retired gentleman farmer. They had a big garden with red, yellow, and black raspberry bushes, as well as grapes, and all kinds of vegetables. They also had several acres of corn in back of the house and kept a cow.

One of my earliest paying jobs was milking Uncle Oscar's cow, which I did every morning at around five, and then again at around five or six in the afternoon. I became quite proficient at this art. In return for these services, my uncle gave me an occasional dime. I don't know whether he had acquired this unique habit from reading about John D. Rockefeller, Sr., who was wont to hand out a dime now and then, but whatever the cause of this generosity, it seemed like quite a bit of money at that time, and I was grateful. The one luxury Uncle Oscar and Aunt Susie pursued was to buy a Buick every year. It was never any other car; it was always a Buick, and always every year. My Uncle Oscar was an early disciple of obsolescence and the need for obsolescence in order to build better and more modern cars. The first thing he would do when he bought his car was to cut down the backs of the front seats, hinge them, equip his car with mosquito netting, and go on a vacation trip with Aunt Susie, always around the same lake—Lake Michigan. He was quite punctilious about this and never went any-place else. During these absences from his home, I more or less, together with my father, took care of his place, milked the cow, enjoyed rich milk rather than skim milk, and we were able to use his icebox, which was something we didn't have.

Uncle Oscar had built another house across the street from his in Sandwich. It was heated by a potbellied stove in the livingroom and a range in the kitchen. There were no indoor toilet facilities. He left it quite unfinished and the basement had an earthen floor. It was into this house that my father and his family moved in May of 1925. I should add that Uncle Oscar had apparently been quite a man about town in Sandwich. He held for a while the position of alderman, and he either gave or arranged to have a piece of land along the main shopping street along the railroad track set aside as a park to which his name was attached for some years. I learned much later that although he was a respected citizen of Sandwich, he lived on the wrong side of the tracks and really didn't belong to the small handful of people who ran the community of Sandwich, who acted as the moral guardians of the youngsters and who, in general, saw to it that the town was a decent place in which to live.

My father's third brother was named Bruno. His young life is a bit of a mystery. He stayed in Chicago, but unlike his older brother Oscar, did not end up with wealth. Instead, he turned toward radical things and apparently became a member of the IWW (Industrial Workers of the World), called the Wobblies at that time. Bruno remained a shadowy figure as far as I was concerned. My father and mother seldom talked about him. There appeared, every so often, in Uncle Oscar's house some people who had had some relationship with Uncle Bruno. However, Uncle Bruno suffered a tragic end. He was jailed. Whether this was because of his radical activities in the burgeoning labor union movement—this was the time of the Haymarket riots in Chicago—or whether it was because of a woman, I was not able to find out. In any event, he committed suicide in jail in Chicago. So here were two brothers: Emil the elder and Bruno the third, who were kept in the background so far as we children were concerned. We were not supposed to know about them; they would obviously only throw a bad light upon us.

My father was the youngest of the four brothers. Raised in the U.S., he spoke English fluently. He apparently acceded to the wishes of his aged, widowed mother to take her back to her homeland before she died. This he did sometime around 1910 or 1911. He settled with his mother in Marienburg, a lovely town on the border between East and West Prussia. Shortly thereafter he met an attractive German girl who was eighteen years his junior. In 1912 they were married. Europe was on the brink of World War I.

In 1913 the delta of the Vistula lay peacefully under the warm sun of summer and the fogs and snow of winter. In the summertime the *pewit* made the loudest noise with its cry of "Kibitz" as he and his relatives circled endlessly over his nest in the reed-covered swamps of the Vistula delta. The bees gave him little competition and occasionally the lowing of a cow could he heard. There were of course no automobiles to disturb the silence of the summer, and in the winter horse-drawn sleds did not at all disturb the peace of the countryside with the jingling of their bells. There was, of course, as there always has been in the Vistula delta, some apprehension about the war because of political developments, but the dark cloud, as proverb had it, was no larger than a man's hand.

It was here that I was born on March 7, 1913. The exact spot was a little red house on a street called Brick Alley in the town of Marienburg on the right bank of the Nogat River, which forms the easternmost mouth of the Vistula. Marienburg's claim to fame was a huge castle built by the Teutonic knights in the fourteenth century. Hugging the river, it was surrounded by a great moat. There were three things about this castle that made a lasting impression on me. Inside was a large, stuffed fish—some people called it a whale. The second was a beautiful mosaic carving of the Virgin and Child on the wall away from the river from which one day the hand of the Virgin fell. It required the skill of the Egyptians, so my father told me, to restore the hand to its proper place. The third was that of the many beggars who stood along the moat and begged passersby to drop a coin into their outstretched hats. I can also remember a wonderful toy store whose name I can recall to this day. It was Gerlach's, and what a wonderland it was for a little boy who could at least look at the hobby horses, even if he couldn't own one, for my father was not a rich man. The youngest son in a large family in whose veins flowed both German and Slavic blood my father had not fallen heir to the sizeable lands of his forebears.

War broke out in 1914. My father, now married and with two small children, me and my sister Christine, remained in Germany. He never explained his reasons for staying. But I suppose the fact that he had a German family, that he probably had an American passport, and the U.S. was not in the war, caused him to stay.

My earliest childhood recollection was that of waking in the middle of the night and seeing the sky to the east as red as if on fire. Frightened, I learned from my parents that this was the reflection of the battle raging in the Masurian Lakes. I remember the terror I felt hearing the stories of the advancing Russians. They were stopped by the old Field Marshall von Hindenburg, who was to serve the last years of his life as president of his country, with Hitler as chancellor. In any event, my father, deciding that the city was no place to be during the war, took his wife and two children to the country where he bought a small farm.

My childhood was spent on this little farm in a village called Half City, "Halbstadt." My recollections of this village are still very clear. It lay on the Nogat River whose waters were contained by a dam that had been built to protect against the spring floods. The dam, which protected us and our neighbors—a handful of people that made up the village of Halbstadt—played an important role in my boyhood days. On the side facing us grew a weed called "Sauerramph," a kind of sorrel. It tasted good and we used to pick it and eat it. The river also supplied us with fish. I can still remember, as a little boy, the pleasant sensation of fear and anxiety about reaching the top of the dam and looking down at the river. We also went swimming here. Much of my time was spent in playing games.

It was here where I encountered my first sexual experience. I was eleven, maybe ten and she was a year or two older. Our families were neighbors. They were farming families and their chores allowed them little time to worry about the youngsters except when they were fretting or ill. So it was that the children spent the long summer days playing games that reflected the environment in which they lived. As their fathers and mothers farmed, so did the children.

As children we had our make-believe farms along one of those sandy roads, some distance from the farms of our parents. Here we marked off fields, made believe that some were planted to wheat, some to rye, and others were just plain pastureland. Our horses and cows and pigs were small shells collected on the sandy banks of the nearby river—big ones for horses, white and black ones for cows, and smaller ones for pigs.

All day long we played the role of farmers, taking the horses out and giving them imaginary tasks like plowing the fields. We pretended to sow grain using fine white pebbles. We harvested and even did the threshing. We traded horses and cows and sold pigs. There were also fairs to which we went, just like our elders.

Of course, all of this took place to the accompaniment of constant chatter, the wisdom of the very young. We made comments about the animals, the fields and the neighbors. Sometimes there were as many as five or six of us at play, but more often only two. And sometimes one would even find oneself alone.

So it happened that we had driven the cows into the barn and it was time for milking. In the course of this chore she remarked in all innocence that her brother could be milked and she asked if I *could* be milked, too? I was astonished at her question, since the idea had never occurred to me, nor did the analogy seem plausible. But she persisted with her question and said she wanted to find out. When I dropped my shorts she shouted with glee that I was like her brother and that she would show me how it was done. I backed off, scared!

School in Halbstadt was a mixture of fun and fear. Fun because we were a very small group of boys and girls and it was fun to play our games and learn under the stern tutelage of Herr Porsch. He was a rather remarkable man and we were all afraid of him, for he did not hesitate to use the stick when one of us had disobeyed him or had done something wrong. However, there was one special occasion and I still remember the date—it was September 19. It was his birthday and on that day we all brought some little token of appreciation to Herr Porsch. The most affluent brought a live chicken or even a goose or a duck. Those less able to make so bountiful a birthday gift brought some eggs and perhaps a fresh fish, just caught in the Nogat River. And those who couldn't afford anything at all brought flowers. Herr Porsch acted, on each of his birthdays, as if it were the greatest surprise of his life, and accepted each gift graciously. Then after tucking the gifts away, he would declare that school was over, after which we went on our annual outing, usually along riverside and had a fun picnic.

One of the better and more enjoyable episodes of our days in school was the fact that Herr Porsch, during the spring, summer and fall months, when we went to school (our school system was different from that of the United States), would designate someone each week to make a collection of flowers, wild flowers, weeds, et cetera, and bring them to school. They were kept fresh in a rain barrel from which he extracted them at a certain time of day and held up each of the plants for identification by the students. This taught me a good deal about flora and I have never ceased to be interested in flowers.

There were the occasional trips to Marienburg, the big city. This was accomplished by horse and buggy, although oftentimes we walked to make it easier for the little horse, which was named "Wachtel," the name of a bird in German. This little faithful horse took us to Kalthof, across the river from Marienburg, where we parked Wachtel and the buggy in a stable, then crossed the bridge to Marienburg, past the castle and the statue of the Alte Fritz, Frederick the Great, and did our shopping. Since we were living at that time in the Free State of Danzig and there was a toll barrier that separated Marienburg from the area in which we lived, we had to pass through Polish sentries. Smuggling was rampant and since we were loaded with coffee and other purchases we scurried past these inspectors as quickly as possible.

It was not all fun. There developed early a strained relationship between my father and me that lingered for the rest of his life. Perhaps it was that he was too old to understand me and the rest of the family, which by 1921 had grown to four: two sisters and one brother. Perhaps it was my fault. My relationship with him was not a close one, which probably accounts for the fact that I learned very little from him about his ancestors and his past.

We survived the war because we lived on a farm, small as it was. Frequently my father butchered a pig in the fall, an operation in which I helped. Nothing was wasted, which was quite a feat since we had no refrigeration. The hams and loins went into the chimney to be smoked. The rest of the meat was pickled in brine or turned into sausage—blood, liver, and bologna sausages. Vegetables were put in the cellar where it was cold, as were the apples and pears. Our hens laid eggs and I rode a bicycle daily to a neighboring village to bring back a huge round peasant bread.

But these were trying days for the Germans. Famine swept the cities and Herbert Hoover made his reputation as the man who helped save the starving Germans. My father decided that his fortunes would not turn for the better and made the move that brought us to the U.S. in May of 1925. We had a short stay in Kalthof before we could book passage on the *Baltic American Line*. It was enough time for me to fall in love with a little girl named Anna Luchs.

# Sandwich—the Making of an American

My Uncle Oscar helped my father and family to come to America. Our destination was a little town in the Midwest, sixty-five miles southwest of Chicago. It was a charming place on the "hard road," Route 34, leading to Carl Sandburg's city. It boasted a population of roughly two thousand people, most of whom made their living in Sandwich itself. It had two banks, a post office, one hospital, a lumber yard, five or six churches, three schools, a small library, a movie house, a factory manufacturing agricultural machines, two or three grocery or "dry goods" stores, one haberdashery, a hardware store, and a bakery. The ice man came around regularly, stopping whenever a sign in the front window indicated one was out of ice. A more ominous sign in the window was red and said "SCARLET FEVER! KEEP OUT!" Once a day the silver Zephyr of the Chicago, Burlington, and Quincy Railroad roared through the middle of town on its way to Denver. Right near the railroad tracks was an old hotel that had seen better days. Lovely elms made arches over the unpaved streets.

Our principal sources of news were the *Chicago Tribune,* owned by Colonel Robert McCormick, the *Aurora*

*Daily Beacon News,* and the weekly *Sandwich Free Press.* My family subscribed to *The Prairie Farmer* and I bought with the first money I earned a subscription to *The American Boy.* Zane Grey and James Oliver Curwood were my favorite authors, with Booth Tarkington a distant third. Theodore Dreiser's *The American Tragedy* made a powerful impression on my young mind and I read and reread the novel, which I borrowed from our public library a number of times. A movie titled *The Road to Ruin* was about illicit love, but today would probably get a PG rating and be considered very tame.

Radio, frequently still powered by batteries, which had to be charged periodically, moved from infancy to adulthood. Every Sunday afternoon found much of Sandwich listening to the "Lady Esther Serenade" featuring the Waltz King—no, not Johann Strauss, but band leader Wayne King, from the Aragon Ballroom in Chicago, and Jan Garber from the Trianon. WLS Chicago served up delightful country music and WGN broadcast the games of the Chicago Cubs. Once a year, in September, Sandwich celebrated its annual fair, which promoted itself as the oldest fair in the state of Illinois. There I exhibited my bantams and rabbits and even won a few prizes.

We arrived in Sandwich, Illinois, at midnight on May 12, 1925. The Chief of Police was there to meet us and take us to our American home. My uncle turned over the house that he had built for us and said, "Here you are, now you're on your own."

It was barely half finished. I slept in what should have been the bathroom. In winter the one window was frozen shut. I recall making designs on the frozen pane. My sisters had the second bedroom and my brother slept with our parents in the master bedroom. The privy was outdoors, reached by a board walk under which the rats

13

scurried. When it was too cold, we used a chamber pot that we kept on the stairs leading to the unfinished second floor. The only heat we had came from a potbellied stove in the living room and another kitchen stove.

The future was to be very difficult for my father. As far as I have been able to determine he never held a regular job. To be sure, he did some farming, but his health was always rather precarious. I recall, while still in Germany, hearing him scream with pain. He may have had stomach ulcers. Given to dreaming of the pot of gold at the end of the rainbow, he now realized that he would have to go to work. His first job was in a laundry at the local hospital. I still recall rather vividly going there after school to see him and remember seeing the bloody sheets and towels that he was washing. Obviously he felt this type of work demeaning and after a short time he found a job in a foundry of the Sandwich Manufacturing Company. Here he did backbreaking labor and it was only his wiry constitution and his doggedness that saw him through. I remember his coming home dirty, with a lunch pail, clothes filthy, and yet after getting cleaned up, he would show us how he could chin himself on the door frame some twenty-five or fifty times, which we all admired greatly. It was my mother who took over as my father grew older and was less able to help. My aunt and uncle continued to pursue their placid lives, taking their annual trips around Lake Michigan in the Buick. My Uncle Oscar was a diabetic and lived with the help of insulin. My Aunt Susie had a stroke that left her bedridden for the rest of her life. Here my mother stepped in and became the good Samaritan. For very little remuneration she took care of two invalids, the most difficult of which was my Aunt Susie, who had to be turned over in bed—she was still a woman of considerable

14

weight. And this was a very, very tough job indeed. Eventually, my uncle was also bedridden and she then had two patients to take care of.

We all grew up in Sandwich. It was a novel experience not to know the language, but it didn't take too long for all of us to pick up English and to move ahead rather rapidly in the school system of this little midwestern town. I know what it is like to be a member of a minority. I could not speak English and when I started in junior high school in the seventh grade, I was of course a minority of one. I was so different from all the rest. I was teased and baited: I can recall the time when someone, during recess, put a chip of wood on his shoulder and said that I should knock it off, which I did. I got a punch in the nose, since I didn't know what the significance of the chip on the shoulder meant. However, I learned fast and in no time I was able to hold my own with the others whose native tongue was English.

It was here in Sandwich where I met my father's older brother, Uncle Emil. I was intrigued by him. He showed me some diaries that he kept and told me that they were in Latin, which was undoubtedly true, because I could not read them, not having had Latin yet. I also grew somewhat resentful at the treatment my Uncle Oscar accorded my father and, to a lesser extent, my mother.

It was a period of growing up; some of it was very pleasant and much of it less so. This was the time when, as I got ready for high school, the automobile became a more commonly used vehicle and replaced the horse and buggy. If you didn't have an automobile then you were sort of a stick-in-the-mud. Hence, it was necessary, as my interest in girls grew, to find someone who had a car. Obviously I couldn't afford to have one. Girls preferred, as they still do today, men with cars.

There were two people who had a remarkable influence on my young life at that time. The first was a teacher in junior high school where I started my schooling in the United States in the seventh grade. Her name was Mary Jackson. She was a very attractive woman with but one shortcoming—I thought her legs were too large. However, I felt a kind of puppy love for her and I did whatever she asked me to do. I recall one time when she was telling us that it was faster to multiply 19 times 248 by multiplying it by 2 and adding a zero to it, then taking off 248. I maintained it wasn't any easier if I could have a piece of paper, and I demonstrated that I could do it faster by multiplying it by 19! Mary Jackson had a profound influence, as I said earlier, on my early U.S. schooling. I recall that she gave a pair of bookends to me when I graduated from junior high school, which I still treasure, with the Indian on a horse at the end of the trail looking into the sunset.

I recall also how jealous I was of one of the more elegant men about town who was much older than she, to say nothing of myself, and who dated her. I imagined all sorts of dire things he was doing to her and that violated my sense of what was right and wrong. I therefore had no use for Bill, who was a banker.

I had jobs almost from the time of my arrival in the United States. I mowed a number of lawns, the largest of which belonged to Judge Latham Castle, who remained a good friend until his death in 1986. He was living in what had been his mother's home, with a huge lawn. Of course we had only hand mowers at the time and I got two dollars for the job, which took me all day. This was the same Latham Castle, who gave me my one and only experience with Illinois politics. I helped launch him on a long political career by campaigning for him on his first and successful run for the office of State's Attorney of DeKalb County. My job consisted of accompanying him on a tour of all the little towns of the county and distributing flyers with his picture on them that said "Vote for Latham Castle." I cheated on him a bit. Weary after so many hours of jumping in and out of the car, depositing flyers in the stores of each town, I deposited a big bunch of them in a culvert where they presumably rotted in time. Fortunately, this act did not prevent him from getting the job, which was to lead in the years ahead to a top position in the Illinois state government, and finally to his being appointed as a federal circuit court judge.

I had a number of smaller lawns, including one, for reasons which I will never know, I completely neglected. The superintendent of the high school was a man named Lynn G. Haskins. He asked me one time, before leaving for his summer vacation in Wisconsin, to take care of his rather small lawn. Since I ordinarily could be depended upon to carry out a task I had assumed, I could not account for the fact that I neglected his lawn completely, and to my great horror, one or two weeks before his return, when I went to look at it, it looked like a hay field. It took me and a scythe several hours to cut it, rake it up, and then try to make it look like a lawn. He never gave me the job again.

When I started in High School I came under the influence of a man who also has remained my friend for life. Carl Thokey was from Racine, Wisconsin, where he lives today. He was a livewire teacher of mathematics and, more importantly for me, the debating coach. I fell completely under his spell and became a star debater, the anchor man for the affirmative team, never lost a single debate, and won the state championship in Illinois. In 1931 the topic for debate was "Resolved, that chain stores

17

are detrimental to the public welfare!" I argued on the affirmative side, which did not hurt my standing with Wilbur Feehan, the genial manager of the Atlantic and Pacific, the first chain store to invade the private enterprise world of Sandwich, Illinois.

Carl Thokey invited his debating team to his home where we played ping-pong with him and his wife. I was never able to beat either one. Carl Thokey had a joyous reunion with his former pupil when I became ambassador and had my swearing-in ceremony in May of 1969. It was a delight to see him and to see him actually so little changed, although his first wife had died in a tragic accident and he had married her sister.

I already mentioned earlier how important it was to have an automobile, in order to rate with the girls who became increasingly interesting to me. This was the time when Ford dominated the young automotive industry. In my senior year I finally persuaded my mother to let me buy a car, if I had the wherewithal. From Charlie Jones, a local dealer, I bought a very old Model T for twenty-five dollars. I learned very quickly, to my dismay, that it had no brakes. I blew two tires coming onto the "hard road." Fortunately for me, there was no traffic, but unfortunately my mother, upon seeing the dilapidated vehicle, made me take it right back to Charlie Jones. I was not to own a car of my own until after I was married and living in New York City.

I recall very vividly one episode where my great buddy and constant companion, Artie Killey, and I dated a couple of girls, not because we particularly liked them but because—quite crassly—the father of one of them had a shiny Model A Ford, which he permitted us to use one evening to go to Aurora, the largest city near us. We went to Exposition Park to dance. It was a perfectly pleasant, harmless evening. I was the driver. We had no hard liquor. In fact I never tasted hard liquor until I was well out of college. Nor did we smoke. We had a good time dancing, and somewhere around midnight returned to the parking lot where I had left the car. We all got into the car—Artie and his date in the back seat and my date and I in the front.

There were practically no cars around us and I turned on the lights and backed up. I'm afraid I stepped on the accelerator a wee bit too hard and the next thing I knew the car was literally rearing like a horse, standing on its rear wheels with the front up in the air. I had backed into a stanchion, a creosoted pole of some sort that refused to yield to the little Ford. There was a good-sized dent in the back of the car and Artie Killey was bleeding from some cut glass. We were able to navigate, however, and return home. And then we did the most cowardly thing we could possibly have done. We allowed my date, the daughter of the man who owned the car, to explain to her father what had happened, while we sneaked away and did not face the music. Needless to say, that was the last time—and the only time—that I dated that girl.

We had dances in the gym, the athletic arena of the high school. Nearly everyone came single and danced with any girl available. In the stands sat the moral guardians of the town. I recall one Saturday morning—after a Friday night dance—while washing the windows of the Sandwich State Bank, being accosted by the president of the bank and being admonished for dancing too close with my partner. "Young fellow, we keep a distance of six inches between partners when dancing!" he said in all seriousness.

I also recall the first aspirin I ever took. Ever since I can remember I suffered from headaches—apparently an inheritance from my mother. One night I came to one of our high school dances looking pale. Maude McDonald, one of two English teachers, asked me if I was all right. I confessed to a headache, whereupon she gave me my first aspirin, a form of medication frowned upon by my mother. But it cured my headache. These headaches were to plague me until I was nearly sixty years of age, when a doctor who had been the director of the medical unit of the State Department suggested a combination of two pharmaceutical products taken regularly, that miraculously cured my headaches.

One of my teachers in high school, Petey Main, was a pretty, perky, slightly bow-legged lady, who taught French and Latin. I took French from her and soon found myself head-over-heels in love. I was in her classroom literally every day after classes were over, helped her clean the blackboard, and worshiped the ground she walked on. My greatest thrill came when, on March 7, 1931, in my senior year on my birthday, she took her French class to Chicago by train to see a performance of Molière's *Le Bourgeois Gentilhomme*. Although spring was just around the corner, it started snowing as we boarded the train in Sandwich and by the time we reached Chicago the snow was three or four feet deep. We wallowed in the heavy snow—there were no taxis to be had—and I of course was the great protector of my beloved French teacher. She took us to a hotel where we all went to public washrooms and dried our feet, and then mushed on to see a delightful performance of that great comedy by Molière. The day was thoroughly satisfying since I was able to demonstrate my ability as the protector of the smaller, but I regret to say, somewhat older woman.

Yes, the four years at Sandwich Township High School were both sweet and bitter.

On the sweet side—I found it easy to make it to the top of my class, whatever the subject matter. There were the extracurricular activities—debating with Carl Thokey as the peerless mentor, the trips, the successes. There were the opportunities to act in school plays—I even had the lead in several. The companionship of excellent teachers. I have already confessed my adoration of Mary Jackson in Junior High—and the incomparable Petey Main. There was also Betty Mesenkop, a tall, angular woman, not beautiful, but a lovely smile, and always ready to help with any problem.

Among those I remember most vividly were the two janitors—"Pummy" Heusinger and "Kate" Hough. It was Kate Hough, the fireman and lawnmower of Sandwich Township High School who provided me with an insight into the glories of the past—more perhaps than any teacher! Kate, always in overalls, and frequently unshaven, belonged to the Book of the Month Club! Whenever the latest arrival was in his hand, we met in the furnace room of STHS and discussed its merits. Kate had an inveterate thirst for knowledge and he found in me a kindred soul. Kate also taught me how to play tennis on the two rather poor courts we had. And then there was always Bill the Greek's, an old-fashioned ice-cream parlor where we could sit hours on end consuming a root beer float. And Dick Holland, the young owner of Holland's drugstore, perhaps the most politically minded of my older friends. These were the days when you either loved or hated FDR! Sandwich, with very few exceptions, hated him.

I have already mentioned my constant companion during my high school years, Artie Killey, the youngest son of a poor family living just a few steps from the CB&Q Railroad tracks.

Artie was one of the neatest persons I ever knew. Decked out in white flannels, blue blazer, and straw hat we walked the two or three miles in the summertime to the fairgrounds to dance. A dime a dance—three for a quarter! What fun!

And we went to the movies together. Our movie house stood on Railroad Street, flanked by the firehouse on one side and a dry goods store on the other. The theater was, for my teen years, the main source of entertainment in Sandwich. It sat squarely near the double tracked CB&Q, on which the aluminum-sheathed flyer thundered through the town, and the new concrete road, always referred to as the "hard" road, on which the cars and trucks, still few in number but increasing every day, were moving on their way to and from the big city.

The owner of the theatre was a man named Frank Bogert. When he died it was amazing how little was known about him. No one knew for sure from where he had come. It was most likely that he had come from the big city, bringing his wife and adolescent son with him. He proceeded to rent a frame house on the wrong side of the tracks, where he and his small family lived quietly. He obviously had had experience with show business because he knew how to procure films and how to run a projector. With a loan, which he persuaded the bank in town to give him, he bought what had been the meeting place of a lodge. It is no longer clear to me whether it was the Moose or the Lions or the Elks. In any event, the lodge had found a better place to hold its meetings above the fire house, which made their old quarters available to Bogert. With a minimum of renovation he opened the movie house.

If Bogert was the main character, Mr. Wood, the pianist, was far better known to the audience that came to the movies. He had another enterprise that occupied most of his time. This was the running of the only hotel in town. However, it was generally believed that his wife, who was about twice his size, was the more dynamic person and actually ran the enterprise. What Wood had that two thousand of his neighbors envied him for was the ability to play the piano without a note in front of him. When he walked down the aisle with his wooden stride, a hush fell on the crowd and everyone knew that the performance was about to begin. Mr. Wood played mood music—music to accompany an artillery charge, music to make a love scene even more tender, and music to draw tears from eyes already ready to respond to the sadness that was revealed on the screen.

Then there was the girl in the cashier's cage. She was a graduate of the local high school, a pretty blonde of Swedish extraction, who had a figure which caused men to turn around and look twice. She was friendly with everyone. She carried on a lively banter with all of her customers, including even the president of the bank.

Standing in the lobby of the theatre was Paul, the popcorn man. No one who knew the movie house and its performances of those days will ever forget him, for no one ever entered without first stopping to buy a bag of the fresh popcorn, which he sopped with melted butter and sprinkled with salt from a large shaker.

The bill of fare of our movie house never varied greatly. Place cards carrying the program for the week were displayed in all the stores, in return for which the proprietors were given two complimentary tickets a week. The *pièce de resistance* was offered for the first time at the Sunday matinee, drew its greatest crowd on Sunday night, and was again offered on Monday. On Mondays the crowd was small but more select—these were the best people in town. They were busy on Sunday with church, a visit with relatives and the church social in the evening. They came on Monday to see what the house had to offer, and as we will see later, to make known to their fellow townsmen their interest in the morality of the place. On Tuesday, the crowd was apt to be somewhat smaller, consisting largely of out of towners who had missed the earlier showings.

Wednesday was dime night. An old film or something that could not be shown in the bigger movie houses of the major cities was offered to all who could produce a dime. Youngsters and oldsters from far and near came to enjoy the chief offering of the evening.

Thursday and Friday were class B stuff, with small crowds. But this was the time for the lovers or, better still, the neckers, especially on Friday night.

While the amorous actions of the young lovers on Thursday or Friday night were more often than not limited to a gentle holding of hands, there was no denying the fact that the dark, the warmth and the exotic influence radiated from the emoting on the silver screen caused many a sigh. The movie house was undoubtedly the place where many an adolescent male had his first electrifying experience with sex. Generally, this was a harmless enough experience, although frequently the sigh that could be heard was not the effect of the scene on the screen but rather the result of too much petting. However, it should be kept in mind that all this petting or necking, as it was called then, was a one-handed operation, for in the other hand there was always the popcorn bag. It was an art that was acquired, but everyone of the youngsters who attended continued to eat popcorn without the use of a second hand.

Nonetheless, looking back upon these nights in the

movie house, morality was rather high. The guardians of the morality of the theatre were the police chief on the one hand and the best people in town on the other. The police chief, and he was always called police chief even though he was the only policeman in town, and had no Indians, was a stolid man in a dark blue serge suit. What distinguished him from other citizens was a bulge, which no one mistook for anything but the butt of his gun. He wore no uniform and he made his beat on foot. Before and during showings at the theatre he stationed himself at a discreet distance from the entrance, occasionally coming to chat with the popcorn man. But he was always there as a warning to ruffians or the occasional drunk, who would be stopped from entering the house.

The "best people" in town were the president of the bank, the district attorney, and the president of the Sandwich Manufacturing Company. They lived on the right side of the tracks in fine homes and their youngsters, of course, like other youngsters from the wrong side of the tracks, attended showings at the movie house. It was never quite clear how the best people ran their intelligence network. It was eerie in fact, though, that they always seemed to hear or always seemed to know when there was some transgression. Invariably the transgressor was called to task the following day by his employer and was told that young people did not dance cheek to cheek or did this or did that. It was surprising how effective this suasion was in maintaining a high standard of morality, given the fact that the theatre was the most obvious attraction in this small town of two thousand.

The movie house enjoyed its greatest popularity in the twenties and early thirties. With the arrival of the "talkies" and the increase in the number of cars, our local theatre began to lose customers with every year that passed. The great city of Chicago, with its splendid Hollywood temples, its double features, its presentation of live performers, like the great Wayne King or Jan Garber and his orchestra, or Hollywood stars between movies, was too great an attraction for people who could now reach the great city. What brought about a hasty end to our movie house, however, was the death of its owner, Frank Bogert.

One night during a show with nearly a full house, the screen suddenly went black, the sound (by now talkies were also at our theatre) went dead and there was a distinct smell of smoke. There was no panic but people filed out quickly, to see in a very few minutes the body of Frank Bogert carried from the projection booth. It was never clearly determined what had caused the fire, and indeed the fire did no great damage. However, apparently the fumes from the burning celluloid had asphyxiated the owner. For years the theatre stood empty, its sign outside not illuminated. There was never another theater in Sandwich.

The spiritual side of my young life in Sandwich was supplied by one of the churches—the Congregational. I drifted, or was pulled into it by the guardians of Sandwich's morality. The old minister had established a reputation for being violently anti-German during World War I and I almost left the church as soon as I entered its membership. His replacement was a fine young minister who made Sunday mornings both uplifting and pleasant. I attended Sunday School and sang in the choir. At a number of church socials I was invited to declaim or orate. I still remember my stirring rendition of "A Message to Garcia" and the ringing "Crown of Gold" speech of William Jennings Bryan. Artie and I rode our bicycles everywhere—even to Aurora, twenty-five miles away—to buy a rayon sports shirt at the five and dime and then slacken the thirst at Bill the Greek's.

But it wasn't all pleasant! One of our high school heroes was the sturdy son of the baker in town. We all knew that he broke the rule of "no smoking," but when he carried the ball, it was frequently for a touchdown. I wanted to play football, but my mother saw one scrimmage and said, "Never again!" But to be part of it I even became water boy for a while, carrying drinking water to the athletes in between plays. This always seemed sort of demeaning. Sandwich played basketball in the "Little Ten," but it was even smaller towns, like Waterman and Hinkley, that won the tournaments at the end of the season.

There was a small golf course between Sandwich and Somonauk, our neighbor to the west. I supplemented my earnings by caddying for the bankers, the lawyers, and the officials of the Sandwich Manufacturing Company. It was at this golf course that I saw a horrible accident. The son of the local police chief flipped a cigarette butt into a trough, thinking it was water—it was gasoline—and in a flash one of the caddies was enveloped in flames. He lived but was debilitated for life.

And then there were the girls! Although I was not bad looking, but didn't have any athletic prowess, I was a star debater. But worst of all was the lack of a car—the guys who had the cars had it made. Oh, we got around it somehow. We befriended guys who owned cars and double dated. But it was always a job—you had to work to get wheels.

There were girls, some very pretty and desirable indeed. And sure, there was experimental sex, but when you didn't have a buggy and met your girl friend at her home, where you took her back after the evening's entertainment, her virginity usually remained intact.

Although I had a crush now and then on a gal, I left STHS after four years with no lasting attachments and no broken hearts. I believe, in retrospect, that I lavished the greater part of my affections on "older women," albeit this was all but once unrequited!

Sandwich summers were hot but beautiful. The whole Midwest with its fields of corn, great barns and silos, was beautiful. And in the fall, the whole countryside was alive with the singing of the crickets. Growing up in this kind of atmosphere was sweet. Bittersweet!

I mentioned earlier that I started working almost immediately after arriving in Sandwich. When I was thirteen years old I applied for and got the job of janitor at the Sandwich Bank, which stood at the corner of Main and West Streets. The work of janitor required that every morning, at the crack of dawn, I had to hop out of a warm bed to a cold, unheated room, leap into my clothes, onto my bicycle and head for the bank. In the winter it was still dark when I went to work, and through the twenty windows of the bank shone two dim lights above its two safes to keep any would-be safecrackers from attempting their dirty business, or if they did, to allow them to be seen by the police chief as he made his rounds.

With the key that had been given me, I let myself in. Then there followed the most awful moment of my life: I had to descend into the basement of the bank to remove the ashes, heap new coals upon the fire, and get the furnace roaring so that it would be nice and comfortable when the doors were opened for business. The basement was part of a subterranean passage under the bank and had many cavelike rooms. I could not get it out of my mind that in the shadows lurked someone who was anxious to rob the bank. If I had been able to think this through logically I would have realized that I was probably the least likely subject to be attacked or to be used in a bank robbery. This did not make the experience any less harrowing, however. In fact there were times when my fear reached a point where I had to ask my father to accompany me down to the basement for this operation of my janitorial chores.

Having gotten the furnace fired up I had to sweep and wash the floors, where I occasionally found a dime or a quarter. I suspected they had been dropped there on purpose to test my honesty. I then completed my chores of cleaning various rooms where depositors took out their safety deposit boxes, the meeting rooms, and the toilets. At just about this time the tellers of the bank arrived. At this point I jumped back on my bike, made a quick stop at Christianson's Bakery for some freshly baked rolls, and hurried home for a quick breakfast and school.

The process was somewhat simpler after school but it was my responsibility to make sure that the fire was banked and that all the doors were locked before night fell. On Saturdays we had our busiest day. This was the time when the farmers come to pay their mortgages, make their deposits, or withdraw their funds. It was also the time when I had to spend the entire morning at the bank with a pail of steaming, sudsy water, a brush at the end of a long pole and a squeegie. I cleaned the windows inside and out, even in the coldest of weather. This was a rather bitter task, for I knew that many of my friends were engaged in activities much more to my liking than what I had to do at the moment. However, the reward was the thirteen dollars that I received at the end of the month and the opportunity to pass some time and have a few words with the best people in town who came to the bank.

There was a time when there was much talk about bank robbers in the general area and indeed, one Saturday morning, it happened. Three men in clothes not distinguishable from those worn by the many patrons in the bank entered, quickly raised kerchiefs from around their necks over their mouths and noses, and flourishing pistols, stated, "This is a stick-up." Everyone's immediate reaction was one of complete shock and total silence. The three robbers ordered the two tellers and the two girls to get down on the floor. Now Alice, a girl of Swedish extraction, was somewhat slow in following orders, and in a most ladylike manner, sat on the floor. One of the three robbers touched her with his foot and said, "Get off your ass and get on your belly—this is not a bank directors' meeting!" Needless to say, she complied with alacrity. The robbers, in true Hollywood fashion, scooped up what money there was in the tellers' cages, left most of the deposits, which were in the safes, and made their way to a waiting car. It wasn't long before they were captured in a field not far from town. However, it was the most exciting day in my life as a janitor at the bank.

Outside of town, in a once-prosperous farm, was a roadhouse. This was during the days of prohibition. This mysterious house sat off the "hard road," old US 34, and was approached by a dirt road. It was forever a source of the liveliest interest to the adolescents of the town. It was known, of course, that the roadhouse was a speakeasy; that this was a place where liquor, which had been made illegal by the Volstead Act, was dispensed to a good many people, including some very reputable ones. It was equally obvious that there was some sort of understanding between the owners of the roadhouse and the police, for it was illegal to sell liquor and the operations of the road house were well known. The question often asked was, "Why was it never raided?"

One of the reasons it probably never incurred the wrath of the county police or the sheriff was that it kept a strict ban on not admitting adolescents. No one under twenty-one was permitted to enter, so all we knew about its operations was what we heard from older young men who had passed that magic age and where now habitues of the place.

Liquor as such was of no particular interest to the adolescents. What was of great interest, however, was the presence of three women at this den of iniquity. They were not girls from town and it was unlikely that they were from the neighboring towns. They probably came from the big city. What, however, was the subject of fervent debate, even at Sunday School sessions, was what these three women did in there. From the habitues we got bits and pieces of information, which were rapidly embroidered and in the retelling became tales of some the most prodigious sexual feats ever performed by female or male! This, of course, led to an even greater interest in the activities of the roadhouse. However, the management never satisfied the curiosity of the excitable adolescent boys.

High school came to an end in 1931, and for all intents and purposes also ended my stay in Sandwich.

*The Reflector*, the annual STHS yearbook, shows me in 1931 as editor-in-chief and a rather callow youth of eighteen. The inscription under my class picture says "ALFRED PUHAN—Prets, Von," which were nicknames I had because of my German background. Below my name follows this entry:

"Debate 2, 3, 4, Oratory 1, 2, 3 Plays 'Pickles'

1—'Once in a Blue Moon' 3—'Hands up' 3—'Cappy Ricks' 4; Latin Club 1,2,4; French Club 3,4; Editor-in-Chief of 'Reflector;' Vice President of Class 1; Glee Club 1,2,3,4; Chorus 1,2,3,4," and ends with this bit of witticism:

"George Washington is dead,
Cicero is dead.
All good men are dying,
In fact, I don't feel so well myself."

The Senior Class Will says "Alfred Puhan wills his excess of grey matter together with his fancy dancing to Kenneth Gengler."

# College

SIX years in Sandwich had taught me a lot. I learned to speak English—so well indeed that I had become a star debater on a statewide winning debate team. I overcame an early language handicap to head my high school class in honors and coming in number one. I learned to act in high school plays, but did not excel in athletics. My mother saw one football game, and promptly forbade my participation. But I was not to be denied totally—I was waterboy for the S.T.H.S. football team. There were many other things this little Midwestern town taught me.

But here I was, near the end of my senior year and I had to make a decision as to what to do next. The farm boys and girls—most of them—returned to their parents' farms and eventually took them over. I realized that a college education was the likely difference between a white- and a blue-collar job. The college I wanted to attend was Northwestern University in Evanston, Illinois. But how to swing this—my parents were poor and unable to help. I had saved up two hundred dollars from the various jobs I held, but the bank failure of 1931 did away with that, or at least postponed the likelihood of getting any part of that.

During this time, the youngest member of a prominent Sandwich family, a sophomore at Oberlin College in Ohio, paid me a visit, bearing a copy of the *Hi-O-Hi*, the college annual book. He told me how his two older brothers, as well as another Sandwichite, had enjoyed and profited from attending Oberlin. I became quite excited at the prospect, but wondered how I could possibly get eight hundred dollars together, which was the minimum required at that time for tuition, room, and board.

Oberlin College, located in Oberlin, Ohio a few miles west of Cleveland, had a student body of nearly one thousand in 1931. It had been a liberal arts college since 1832 and proud of the fact that it was the first college to admit women and even prouder still for having served as a station on the underground route Negro slaves took when escaping from the south on their way to Canada.

Perhaps better known for its conservatory of music—a truly excellent institution—it also boasted of having a school of theology. It had a great collection of fine arts housed in an Italian Renaissance building. Its faculty of some 100 men and women represented an outstanding collection of scholars. Oberlin prided itself in having one faculty member for every ten students. Nearly every department had at least one female professor. Oberlin's library was outstanding. The president in 1931 was Ernest Hatch Wilkins, a distinguished scholar and authority on Dante. The architecture of the college was a mix of old Gothic and new Italian Renaissance, a combination, which, strangely enough, did not clash. There were no fraternities or sororities. In their place were a number of "houses," like Delta, White House, or Manor, whose inmates selected the freshmen they wanted to join them in their second, third, or fourth years.

Athletics were generally arranged to benefit all of the students. Sports were basically intramural, although

Oberlin fielded a football team, which generally won very few games, and a basketball team, which did better. Dan Kinsey was a superb track coach and Oberlin generally did well in running, jumping, and other field events.

Oberlin's faculty included some remarkable personalities. There was the imperious Ruth Lampson, a dowager lady with red hair and ample bosom, who, in English II welcomed a late, well-endowed female arrival with the words, "Well, Miss S———, I see you are busting in late as usual!" Freddy Artz was the Liberace of the History Department, a wisecracking, witty professor of European history, and the author of a book who was later accused of plagiarism. There was George Henry Danton, chairman of the German department, who was accused of having seduced the daughter of the president of a Pacific Coast College, and exiled to China for eight years. Pete Cole was the witty member of the psychology department whose courses were much in demand. Jimmy Hall delivered the very popular and mandatory music appreciation course in the conservatory. Hope Hibbard taught freshmen how to dissect frogs and learn all about the interiors of reptile bodies. And on and on . . .

I arrived in Oberlin, this New England oasis in the Midwest, with a scholarship worth about two hundred dollars, in the fall of 1931. My belongings fit easily in a cheap suitcase. They included a new suit I had bought at the local haberdashery—it had two pairs of pants, one being a pair of knickers, which were popular at that time. The suit was a bargain, since it had been in the store window for quite some time, causing the sun to bleach the front to a slightly lighter color than the back. I recall crossing the campus one day while wearing this suit when a more affluent member of my class saw me and said, "Ye Gods, where did you get this two-toned suit?"

Oberlin had no fraternities, so we lived in buildings, each with its own name. Most of the freshmen lived in Men's Building, a huge four-story affair with wide staircases over which one of our more exuberant classmates rolled down bowling balls. My roommate hailed from nearby Cleveland and soon he and I hitchhiked to Cleveland to spend the weekend with his parents, but not before we had paid a visit to the striptease theater, the Burlesque, downtown.

Those were moments of relief from the rest of the week. I worked hard, knowing that unless I did really well, I probably would not keep my scholarship. Oberlin had at that time a merciless way of grading students—not by giving customary As, Bs, Cs, et cetera, but by rating each member of a class against the rest of the class. Thus I was number one in most classes. If a student transferred to another school or went on to graduate school his standings were then translated into As, Bs, et cetera. The system pitted each student against all the others in the class. The system was abolished after I had left Oberlin.

The curriculum for the first two years at Oberlin consisted of a number of required courses—English, math, a language, science, and some electives. I opted for German as my language requirement, but after the first day in German I, my teacher asked me to stay after class. He inquired where I had obtained my knowledge of German. I told him, of course, that I was born in Germany, but had not spoken German since I was twelve. He promoted me to a more advanced course, and thus I came to the attention of the head of the German Department. More about that later.

Oberlin opened vistas for me. I felt exhilarated by the experience of being with professors and students, many of whom had far more experience than I. I heard my first classical music, a concert by the Cleveland Symphony playing in Finney chapel. I went to my first art gallery at Oberlin, which even then was an outstanding college art museum. I heard distinguished speakers in the chapel from all walks of life.

My social life was fairly circumscribed. We did have, on most week days, one hour of "Rec" (Recreation), an hour of dancing in Peters Hall to piano music after dinner had been served. And then there were the more formal proms with big bands playing for the dances. Dates were not hard to come by since the women at Oberlin outnumbered the men two to one. Many of the girls came from the eastern states and were daughters of parents, who more often than not had graduated from Oberlin. Women had to observe strict rules, particularly the freshmen. They had to be in their rooms by nine or earlier in the evening. However, there were walks in the arboretum, but since this little wooded area by the water reservoir was so filled with smooching couples, there was little privacy. But it was dark and we were young! Cars were taboo on campus so life was pretty well confined to Oberlin's grounds.

To save money I shipped my dirty laundry home each week (or every two weeks) in a cheap container by railroad parcel post. When it came back with the clothes freshly washed and ironed, there were cookies and other goodies packed by my mother. This was always a most welcome contribution to my life at Oberlin—but it was about all my family could contribute.

My grades flourished and at the end of the first semester of my freshman year, I ranked second in my class of roughly 250 students. My parents and I were elated, but I was somewhat deflated when I sought out the dean of men to inquire about my scholarship for the next semester. He praised my scholastic achievements but noted that I had not participated in athletics and Oberlin tried to prepare the "total man." This was astonishing to me since Oberlin prided itself on its scholastic record and played down the athletic program. Indeed Oberlin, then as now, won few athletic contests except in track.

But I was not to be denied. I received some small help and augmented that with all kinds of odd jobs—picking up laundry and taking it to the dry cleaner, babysitting, and even shoveling manure on the lawn behind some girls' dormitories.

My college career began to blossom with my second year. I started to work in a psychology laboratory at very low pay, but which was nevertheless a most helpful addition. I gained confidence and found the courses I took quite easy, and my grades soared.

Sometime during my second year at Oberlin, I was approached on the campus by the head of the German department, a very strange man who, as I said earlier it was rumored, had seduced the president's daughter of a small college in the west. It was said that she committed suicide and he was exiled to China, where he remained for some seven or eight years. There was no question about his brilliance, intellectually and linguistically, but he had a way of embarrassing his students, particularly the women in his classes, with stories such as the following: If, in China, a maiden is discovered nude in the bath, a river, or pond by a man, she placed her hands over her face. In Europe and the USA, he maintained, she would cover her pubic region.

In any event, he told me one day during my sophomore year that if I would major in German and take honors, he would guarantee me a fellowship to do graduate work. Since this was the time—the early thirties—when college graduates were out selling apples, I took, perhaps naively, the path of least resistance, and agreed to major in German.

As it turned out, this choice, which I had reason to question in my immediate post-college days, served two immensely useful purposes. While taking advanced German, when one of my fellow students would read just one or two plays by Schiller, I would read all of his works. At the same time I was free to take electives ranging from astronomy to zoology.

But of far greater importance was the fact that my knowledge of German art, history, and literature, as well as my fluency in the language, were to shape my career long after I left the academic field.

There were two areas in which I did not distinguish myself. The first was physical education, a required course during the first two years. I could not perform on the high bars and on all the other infernal equipment in the gym. Indeed, I fell off the high bar several times to the dismay of the instructor.

The other was music appreciation, taught by a very popular professor in the conservatory to over a hundred students in my class. I came out somewhere in the second half of the one hundred students.

Speaking of music, one of the dividends of becoming a German major was almost mandatory attendance on Saturday afternoons in the home of the head of the German department to listen to the Metropolitan operas introduced by Milton Cross. When you arrived at the professor's home, there was a paper tacked to the door stating, "Come in quietly, take a seat and listen." It was a musical education, even though on beautiful days, some of us longed for the outdoors and the arboretum.

My new digs came rent free when the same scion of

a prominent Sandwich family, who had recruited me for Oberlin, invited me to share his attic room on the third floor of a private house owned by three very old ladies who lived on the second floor. My duties were not onerous. I just had to keep the furnace going in winter and mow the lawn in the fall and spring.

When my roommate graduated at the end of our year together, I invited a brilliant classmate to join me, which he did, for the last two years of our Oberlin stay.

Our garret became quite popular with some of our classmates, who liked to come over and watch some of the girls undress in the women's dormitory next door!

There was one incident that nearly terminated our lease on the garret room. My roommate and I took turns in looking after the furnace. One morning, I was awakened by my roommate, who said in a rather lugubrious tone, "Roomy, our cellar is afloat." Apparently I had failed to shut off the water while filling the pipes and the water had burst a pipe and was threatening the very expensive piano on the first floor of our house—the treasured possession of a teacher of music at the conservatory!

My board and my meals I earned as waiter at May Cottage, a very prominent and popular girls' dormitory. We had a marvelous crew of waiters and favored certain girls with little extras. We ate in our private dining room and, between courses, served in the girls' dining room.

One of my fellow workers at May was a talented voice student at the conservatory. I told him at the end of my junior year—I had made Phi Beta Kappa that year—that I had one remaining ambition: I wanted to become a member of the college glee club, an organization not to be confused with the superb college choir. The trouble was I did not read music and had barely made the Sandwich High School Glee Club.

Admission to the glee club was voted on by members after an audition. With the help of my conservatory friend I sang "Home on the Range," and with a good but untrained bass voice was immediately accepted. The genial director decided that I would do a solo number, a Victor Herbert song titled "A Regal Sadness Sits on Me," with hankies tucked in various parts of my tux and a quartet behind me to accompany me. This was a great hit, oo pecially on tour, with kids in the front rows who loved to hear my *basso profundo* hit the low notes. It was better than "Boo-hoo, You've Got Me Crying Again."

Unfortunately, this same genial director also decided I would sing bass in a quartet. I had trouble with this, since the baritone next to me had a beautifully trained voice, and I invariably slipped into his part.

Disaster struck in Waukegan, Illinois, where we were on our Christmas tour. There was a point in the song where the bass carried the melody while the other three were silent. Unfortunately, I was already with the baritone, and when my turn came to do my solo, I stopped. There was an embarrassing pause until the tenor had the presence of mind to pick up the tune. It was the last time I sang in the quartet!

In my senior year I was quite a big man on campus. I had surmounted the possibility of becoming known as a "grind," a student interested only in studies, since I appeared everywhere—at dances, concerts, and sports events.

I fell in love with a pretty girl two years my junior, but she had a boy friend back home whom she intended to marry when she graduated. I fell in love again with a statuesque gal from the Main Line of Philadelphia, but her parents, and possibly she, too, had other plans. My prospects as a German major did not seem very good.

Although I graduated *summa cum laude* with honors in German, a Phi Beta Kappa, and first in my class, the event for which I will probably be best remembered had little to do with studies, honors, or girls.

It was a spring day in 1935, near the end of my college career. We were all boning up for final exams. Having closed my book while studying in the school library, I stretched and my hands enfolded two of the lamps on the table. Suddenly I was being electrocuted—a current of electricity shot through my body. With superhuman effort I yanked the two lamps out of their moorings and broke the shorted current. The lamp shades came crashing down, spewing glass all over the table and floor. The director of the library came running out of his office and demanded to know what I was doing—a silly question! One of my classmates put me on his bicycle and took me to the campus hangout for a cup of coffee. That evening when I entered the gym, where some athletic event was to take place, I was applauded by an audience that rose to a man, and many even asked for my autograph. The next day the college newspaper headlined its front page as follows: "Yeoman Puhan renovates library!" And that is what—more than half a century later—many of my still-living classmates remember about my career at Oberlin.

Oberlin was an awakening. With its tradition of firsts—women, blacks—it was truly a liberal institution. My association with professors like Freddy Artz, Mr. Fletcher, Ruth Lampson, Mrs. Hubbard, and many others had a profound influence on me. The narrow viewpoint I brought from a little town in Illinois was widened. Although I arrived at Oberlin with my mind nourished by Robert McCormick and the *Chicago Tribune*, I left after four years with more of an Adlai Stevenson outlook. I felt a confidence that I could do things, could learn virtually anything!

The greatest satisfaction I had on graduation day was to see the pride on my mother's face. She managed to get away from her arduous duties of caring for her two invalids and to come to Oberlin. She realized that she and my father had been unable to contribute much to my tuition, board, and room, but she had shown her devotion by doing my laundry and sending me goodies that I shared with my roommates for four years. Now she saw her eldest graduate from a college of renown with high honors. This was a high point in her life and in mine.

# Academe

From a garret room in Oberlin I moved to a garret room in Cincinnati, Ohio. The house belonged to the head of the German department at the University of Cincinnati. He offered the room to me at a very low rent, feeling undoubtedly that he was helping me eke out an existence as a teaching fellow. Since he was the head of the department in which I was a graduate student, I didn't know how to gracefully reject his offer.

I came to the University of Cincinnati on a Taft Memorial teaching fellowship with a stipend of one thousand dollars, which was more money than I had ever seen to that time! I owed the fellowship to the head of the German Department at Oberlin, who had promised me a fellowship if I majored in German. He kept his word, although I had never heard of the University of Cincinnati before. The University of Cincinnati was a municipal institution. Heading it was Roy Walters, a fine administrator. Without being well known at the time in the academic field, it offered a number of possibilities to get a Ph.D. It had a good, if not distinguished faculty. Its principal advantage was that it was located in a city rich in musical heritage. Its orchestra, conducted at the time by Eugene Goosens, was one of the best in the country. Its summer opera season from the zoo was excellent.

The German Department at the University was a strange collection of scholars. The head of the department was a Milquetoast-like character, whose principal interest was Ludwig Tieck, one of the dullest German literary figures I've ever come across. There was a very senior professor, German by birth, who looked like one of the German novelists of the nineteenth century, some of whom he had probably known in Germany. There was a philologist, a gentle young man with a dry wit and a flirtatious wife. And finally there was a heavyset German instructor with whom I shared an office. It was his wont, when both of us were preparing our lessons, to stare across his desk at me and say, "I know what you're thinking." I never learned what he had in mind.

My teaching load—my first experience as a teacher—was not onerous. I taught beginning German, which I found a real joy, since it was the only language course in which you could see real progress, even by the dullest of students. My second course was scientific German for pre-med students. This was an altogether different kettle of fish: the problem was that I knew neither the German nor the English vocabulary of that course. With the help of future doctors we muddled through.

I took courses in German literature, which led to a master's degree in 1937. Much of my free time I spent on other matters.

Cincinnati had much to offer: good music and some good theater. With a thousand dollars I felt rich. Indeed, my first purchase was a small Sears Roebuck radio with a green dial. Many an evening I whiled the time away in my garret room long past midnight, listening to my radio. I'll never forget "Moon River." During my first year as a paying guest of the head of the German Department, I shared a second floor bathroom with the owners. When

I walked through an unlocked door to find the daughter of the owners in all her nude glory, she uttered a shriek, and I had to move my residence to a one-room apartment near the university, which I shared with a fellow graduate student who kept me awake with his loud snoring.

My social life was spent largely with young married couples—young men working hard and bored wives ready for any dalliance. I became a member of a group that included the heir to a great tobacco fortune. Their parties were always noisy and fun. There were serious discussions also and much talk of the future and Adolf Hitler. What was he up to and would there be another war? The Midwest was generally isolationist and the antiwar movement was growing. FDR was suspect and many believed that he was leading us into war.

At the end of my second year—also on a stipend of a thousand dollars—and with an MA tacked on to my AB, I was offered an equal or even greater amount if I stayed on and got a Ph.D. Although by now I was steering a course that would obviously lead to teaching and needed a Ph.D., I felt uneasy about a Ph.D. from the University of Cincinnati, which people elsewhere probably had never even heard of. The University of Wisconsin and Johns Hopkins University were generally considered to have the best German departments at the time.

I cast out a number of lines. Columbia offered me a small fellowship, significantly smaller than what I had enjoyed in Cincinnati. I accepted and in the fall of 1937 moved to the Big City.

New York in 1937 was a wonderful place. The tallest building was still the Empire State. Streetcars, without the smell of diesel, and the subways moved most of the pedestrian traffic. There were plenty of restaurants that served a delicious meal for sixty-five cents, and apartments went for as little as forty-five dollars a month. Horn and Hardart's imposing cafeteria on West Fifty-seventh was a great place for an inexpensive and wholesome lunch. Schraft's, right next door to the Voice of America was also a popular eating place. For a real treat, you went to the more expensive Russian Tea Room, a neighbor of Carnegie Hall.

My home in New York City was a small dormitory room on the top floor of John Jay Hall on the Columbia campus. The staff of the German Department consisted of the chief, a soft-spoken Virginian, who loved to speak German, but could never acquire the proper accent. Once, upon introducing a Swiss scholar, he wanted to say that in his heart he had always admired him. He used the wrong preposition, which came out that he was pregnant with the Swiss professor! There was a pixieish philologist, who used the latest slang in translating medieval epics (knights "biffed" each other in old German epics). A third member of the department was a mumbling Germanist with a strong predilection for anything German and, it was rumored by some of the students, even for Hitler. A fourth professor managed to put most of us to sleep with his sing-song voice. And there was a professor of Dutch, a native of the Netherlands, who kept us awake with his stories of his native land.

The number of graduate students was not large and most of us became good friends. One of them, Henry Hatfield, who became a brilliant professor at Harvard and his charming wife, Jane, have remained true friends for life. Another, a very witty man, who thought all German literature was rather second or third rate, believed the United States ended at the Hudson River. He became a professor at UCLA where he spent the rest of his career, but not before he disposed of his entire German library.

47

Somewhere along the way, perhaps at the end of my first semester, I ran out of money. In desperation I wrote to a professor of German at Oberlin who had befriended me, and he promptly sent me a check for a hundred dollars, with a note stating that I could repay this if I ever felt like it and had the wherewithal to do so. I squeaked through.

The most memorable academic experience of my graduate career at Columbia was attending the lectures of H. A. Korff, the last German exchange professor before the Nazis and the war ended the exchange program. Korff, a brilliant scholar with several books to his credit, always sartorially impeccable, and speaking a beautiful German almost sang when he lectured. When compared to his Columbia colleagues, he was like a thoroughbred among a bunch of plowhorses.

My fascination with him led to a strange mental lapse on my part. As president of the German Club, I invited distinguished Germanists to present monthly lectures. I was to introduce a German scholar from Harvard, a German professor who was to remain in the United States, unlike Korff. When I listed the books written by Korff and attributed them to Vietor, the scholar in residence at Harvard, my audience became somewhat restless, until Professor Vietor tapped me on the shoulder and said in a soft voice, "I wish I could take credit for all those fine books written by Professor Korff."

The most significant event of the seven years spent in academe had nothing to do with academic matters. I got married on November 5, 1938, to Fairfax Judd. I had known her slightly at Oberlin, but never dated her, since she was going "steady" with a classmate and appeared to be heading for marriage with him when she graduated two years later than I from Oberlin.

During my first year at Cincinnati, I traveled to Oberlin to revisit the scene of my undergraduate days. I went by express train from Cincinnati to Cleveland. Before I boarded the train I inquired if I could get off at Wellington, a small town not far from Oberlin, and was told I could. The conductor on the train was amazed when I told him I wished to disembark at Wellington, saying never in the long history of that run had the train stopped in Wellington. Reconciled to going into Cleveland, I, as well as the other passengers were astonished to hear the brakes being applied and the train stop in farming country, just a bit past the tiny Wellington station!

In Oberlin I was visiting with some friends in the campus hangout when Fairfax Judd came in with some girl friends. One of my friends said that if I called her I could probably get a date with her for the prom that night. I called and she accepted. We had a good time.

Fairfax was the oldest of three daughters born to Howard and Vera Judd of Michigan. The marriage of her parents always struck me as just a bit strange. Her father was a very earthy man with a good sense of humor, a man who had failed at farming, but made a success of selling furniture, a job in which he, with wise investments, made more than a quarter of a million dollars.

Fair's mother was very much the opposite of her husband. She was a graduate of Vassar, with interests in politics, theater, and art—subjects which left her husband cold. She was much taken with me and liked to discuss subjects she never discussed with her husband.

Fair was a petite five-foot-one pretty girl with good features, was most photogenic, had a nice figure, a nice smile, and poor feet that troubled her most of her life. She was highly intelligent and had a great deal of courage. And I fell in love with her.

However, it took her inviting me to be her date at her Senior Prom in 1937 to lead to a courtship in the summer of 1937 when I visited her family at a lake cottage in lower Michigan. Although smitten with her, I was not thinking of marriage at that time since I had no job and was barely eking out an existence at Columbia. I had a good many misgivings about my future as a teacher of German with a second war against Germany a gloomy and not so distant prospect.

Nonetheless, as many other young people did and still do today, I threw caution to the winds and, in November of 1938, married Fairfax Judd in a chapel at Saint Thomas's church on Fifth Avenue and Fifty-third Street in New York City.

Our married life began in an old brownstone house on Ninety-sixth Street, just off Riverside Drive in New York. It had bedbugs! I supplemented my earnings as a teaching fellow in night school at Columbia and by working on a dismal project with a young instructor at Teacher's College. Fairfax started to work in lower New York, but the subway, even then, was too much for her.

When the spring semester of 1939 came to an end, I had completed all my requirements for my doctoral thesis except for the written dissertation. I passed five days of grueling exams, and was ready for a job. None appeared before we left New York for Sandwich, Illinois, where we spent an uneasy summer at my mother's home. I recall that summer reading *Gone with the Wind* and listening to the Chicago Cubs' games. The summer could have been idyllic if I had not worried so much about a job, and indeed, our future.

In September 1939 Hitler invaded Poland, and World War II was on. Colleges were not hiring German instructors. At the very last moment, Columbia University came through with an offer of a part-time job at Barnard College, the women's equivalent of Columbia College. With the promise of some teaching in Extension at night, we returned to New York.

At Barnard I faced a lot of young women, most of whom were not greatly interested in German. One young lady invariably spread out the *New York Times* when I tried to explain the not-so-easy mechanics of the German language. I finally suggested to her that she could probably enjoy the *Times* more outside of the classroom, where my lecturing would not disturb her.

I remained at Barnard for two years. My greatest concern during my walks to and from Ninety-sixth Street to Barnard at 118th Street was that my wife might get pregnant, without my having a real job.

However, our social life improved. We joined a number of highly congenial couples, all of them either struggling through postgraduate work or already teaching at Columbia at very meager salaries. We had parties and entertained each other. We had no hard liquor, but occasionally indulged in cheap wine. We all smoked, of course. We went to a Chinese restaurant on Broadway, where for sixty-five cents, we ate what one of my good friends termed "Chinese pablum." We argued and discussed the pressing problems of the time: Hitler and the war; FDR; isolationism. Except for the war clouds, which threatened to engulf the United States and us all, we enjoyed ourselves.

Then in the spring of 1941, I received an offer of a full-time teaching job, an instructorship at a salary of eighteen hundred dollars per annum, at Rutgers College in New Brunswick, New Jersey. I leapt at the opportunity—a real job at last!

But before we could get there Fair came down with

appendicitis. She wept in the hospital, as she said that we could have had a baby with the money it would take to pay for the operation.

Nineteen forty-one to nineteen forty-two—one year at Rutgers was to be my last year in academe. As the youngest member of a staff of four in the German department, I was assigned the most advanced courses given. This was so because the head of the department preferred to teach beginning German to giving lectures on German literature, and the other two members were either unqualified or did not want to burden themselves with the preparation of lectures on Goethe, Schiller, and the nineteenth century German novelists.

My teaching the advanced courses meant that I had to work hard and had small classes. There were few German majors, but the students I had were good and I thoroughly enjoyed them. But we did not like New Brunswick!

During my first semester at Rutgers, on December 7, 1941, Japanese bombs rained on Pearl Harbor and we were at war. The bombs also ended my academic career at the end of the second semester.

Looking back over the years, I enjoyed my brief teaching career at Cincinnati, Barnard, and Rutgers. I believe I was a good teacher. Indeed, Rutgers offered me a fifty-dollar raise to return a second year. Had the war not terminated my teaching, I suppose I might in due time have become a full professor, eventually heading a German department at some college or university. I did not finish my doctoral dissertation, largely because the Virginian at the helm of the German department at Columbia vetoed all my suggestions for a thesis and recommended that I do a thesis on the German verse epic in the nineteenth and twentieth centuries. This poetic form that flourished in the Middle Ages was revived by the German Romanticists in the early nineteenth century and was copied and degraded by a number of poets in the last century. I must have read five hundred or six hundred of such poems and had copious notes, but I never quite figured out what I would do with them. I finally burned them all after World War II and a return to the academic world appeared improbable.

# The Voice of America

**W**ITH the breath of the Draft Board on my neck, I reconciled myself to joining the army, albeit with little enthusiasm. There was my young marriage and a background of isolationism, having grown up in the Midwest where the Chicago Tribune had been my principal intellectual fodder.

Out of the clear blue sky there appeared a telegram at my home in New Brunswick in the early spring of 1942. The rather mysterious message asked me to report to 270 Madison Avenue right away in connection with the war effort. I learned later that it was a questionnaire I had filled out at Barnard College, stating my qualifications in the event of war, principally my knowledge of German and French, that had elicited the request.

Upon my arrival at the above address in New York City, I was met by a disheveled, harassed little man who asked me in a Germanic accent whether I could read two pages he held in his hand. I noted they were in French and German and read a few sentences. He then steered me into a bare room—a radio studio, with a solitary microphone in the middle. He asked me to read the German into the mike, and after a couple of sentences bade me halt and said that I would be on the BBC that night.

I did not know what the BBC was, and after he rather scornfully said it was the British Broadcasting Corporation, I had to ask what it was doing in New York. He explained in some irritation that I was in the studio of the Voice of America, which was using the facilities of the BBC since it had none of its own. I had the afternoon to ponder the events of the recent few minutes since I was not due at the studio until evening.

A word is in order here to explain the origins of the Voice of America (VOA). Our country had never engaged in propaganda. To be sure, in World War I there was some internal propaganda, but essentially propaganda for most Americans was anathema—it meant lying. Propaganda can, of course, be lying, but it can also be truthful. Call it propagation. The church has propagated the faith for centuries.

The British had built a world-wide broadcasting network over the years, chiefly to reach every member of the British Empire. It was thus easy to use available transmitters and studios in Bush House, London, to beam the news and editorial comment to Nazi Germany. The BBC had a policy of telling the truth, good or bad. British losses, British defeats, German victories—it called them as it saw them, and hence established a record for reliability and trust. If you heard it on the BBC, it was true.

Upon our entry into the war in December of 1941, some farsighted individuals saw the need to have America's voice heard. The VOA began under the umbrella of the Office of Strategic Services, the OSS, and my first paycheck came from something called "Shortwave Research, Inc."

When I appeared at 270 Madison Avenue in New York that day in May of 1942, I was really very nearly in at the beginning of the VOA, with which organization I was to spend the next eleven years.

But to go back to that first day of my broadcasting. I watched with some awe as the cast assembled: There was a man whom I recognized as having played in the Fu Manchu movies, a young German who played Nazi roles on radio, and a famous announcer from the Lucky Strike Radio Hour. The director was the same little German who had tested my languages that afternoon.

My role in that first broadcast was to say "London," giving it the German pronunciation, after which one of the stars read an item emanating in London. Next I said "Berlin," in German, and again there followed a news item from Berlin, read by one of the stars.

I worked full time—two shows a day—for nearly a month, at the end of which I received a check for six hundred dollars! I looked at my wife and said, "For one-third of what I got at Rutgers per annum for doing what I could have done at the age of six—this is for me!"

Obviously I performed satisfactorily because I was promoted and allowed to read the entire news item after another announcer did the placing of the item. And indeed, it was not long until the director of the broadcast invited me into the control room to learn production of radio news. I was given a few hand signals: to speed up, to slow down, to cue music. During the middle of the first broadcast as a trainee, the phone rang; the director left the control room and did not return. As I watched the minute hand make its revolutions I grew somewhat apprehensive as to how to end the broadcast. I turned to the engineer who said, "Simple. Make a sign as though you would cut your throat, I'll flip the switch, and we're off the air." From that day I was a producer!

The VOA was transferred to the newly formed Office

of War Information and moved to a building at the corner of Broadway and Fifty-seventh Street in New York. My wife and I left New Brunswick and Rutgers for good. My career as a teacher was over. We found a nice fifth floor apartment on West 110th Street, from which we could see the Cathedral of Saint John the Divine. We bought our first furniture, since up to that time we had lived in furnished apartments.

Although my early duties at the VOA were mainly with the German Desk and German language broadcasts, as producer I was frequently asked to do shows in other languages: for a time I did a midnight to 8:00 A.M. shift.

The VOA was a fascinating organization. Under one roof at Fifty-seventh and Broadway were gathered some of the best minds of Europe—refugees driven out by Hitler. Directives for the broadcasts originated in the OWI headquarters in Washington, D.C., with Elmer Davis, famous news commentator at the helm. However, the VOA was a free-wheeling organization and frequently was ahead of a directive or even not in line with it.

The objective of the VOA in those early war years was simple: destroy the morale of the Nazis in Europe and defeat Japan in the East. Each of the language desks at the VOA had members representing various shades of political opinion—from Habsburg right wing to leftist leanings with strong support of the Soviet Union. In peace time such people might have been at each other's throats, but the common goal of defeating Nazi Germany held them together. This was not to be the case after World War II came to a close.

The German Desk at the VOA was manned by some highly literate men and women, many of whom were Jewish exiles who had managed to escape Hitler's grasp. They were on the whole a quarrelsome and noisy lot.

The Austrian desk, which fought association with the German Desk, had a cast of characters, including a former Austrian general who had fought in Spain against Franco, a future Austrian ambassador to Paris, a man who later became a highly successful public affairs officer in the United States Information Agency, and a Viennese lawyer who had been supported by the last pretender to the Habsburg throne. Suspicion of each other was rife, and position and rank zealously guarded. I recall when I made the mistake of issuing a memorandum and put one of the names above another one who felt he should be listed ahead and therefore felt was being demoted that I caused a first-class crisis!

I enjoyed my association with these highly intelligent, worldly, wise people. As the months went by I received further training in radio by going to CBS, NBC, and Mutual to do what were called "standby shows." These were timeless, dramatic productions, having to do, of course, with the United States war effort, which were produced at the domestic networks, put on glass or acetate discs (we had no tape in those days), and shipped to the BBC in London where they were used whenever the VOA shortwave broadcasts did not go through because of atmospheric disturbances—hence the standby shows.

As I grew more confident among the German and Austrian writers, I also became more critical of their output. While they all shared a deep hatred for the Nazis, they knew little, if anything, about the country of their recent adoption. One of the tasks of the VOA was what was called "the projection of America." But how do you do that if you've never been west of the Hudson?

When my criticism of the scripts came to the attention of some of the German authors I was told, with some vehemence, that I should try writing if I knew so much better. I accepted the challenge and added scriptwriting to my job description. Indeed, I became a name commentator, using the pen name of Alfred Zimmerman, since my own name is rather hard to visualize in German or English. In my commentaries I sought to explain why the United States war effort would eventually doom the Nazi conquest, even though at the time German armies still had to taste defeat.

There were some hilarious moments at the Voice of America. Someone thought we should broadcast Sunday religious programs to the Nazi-heathen Germans. The man selected to read the sermons was a doughty North German, who was usually quite tipsy by the time he was to read the sermon in his whiskey baritone. What ensued was scarcely elevating. On one occasion I read a news item regarding that charming island of Lampedusa. I gave the name of the island with such emphasis that the whole cast broke down in hysterics. The engineer saved the day by "flipping the switch."

On still another occasion, Eleanor Roosevelt stepped off the elevator to record a program and was greeted by a shouting producer with the words, "I can't find my God-damned script!" The wife of the president only smiled.

In 1943 the first Allied victories in North Africa brought thousands of German prisoners of war to our country. Camps were established in the southwest—Oklahoma, Texas, Arkansas, and Mississippi. We conceived the idea of entering the POW camps with a recording van and see if the POWs were interested in sending a message via VOA to their relatives in Germany and Austria. Permission was granted by the military. Accompanied by my Fu Manchu friend, a representative of the military, and a recording engineer, we set out in late 1943 for the southwest.

We left no doubt in the camps we entered that we represented the VOA and not the Red Cross. We made clear that anyone could say virtually anything except "Heil Hitler" and that we would not tamper with their messages.

I do not recall now how many camps we visited, but I remember that we recorded some fifteen hundred prisoners who let mother, wife, sister, or aunt know that they were safe and were looking forward to a speedy end of the war. They probably did not realize that their description of life in the POW camps—their daily ration of butter, eggs, meat, and cigarettes—made some of the best listening bait we could possibly produce.

Not all of our sailing was smooth. I visited a German POW general who greeted me with the Heil Hitler salute and informed me, when I told him what we were doing, that surely I would not expect him to commit treason. We had, however, a pleasant enough conversation, which concluded with his complaint that the mail was not reaching him and his men. When I relayed this to the U.S. camp commander, he replied, "Hell, I don't write to him."

The American camp commanders were a colorful lot. Either too old or too unqualified to go to the front, they were put in charge of the German POWs, whom they adopted as "their troops." I recall a quiet dusk in Texas when I stood with a United States lieutenant colonel who was in charge of that camp, as we heard the a capella singing of the German troops returning from the fields they had been working to their camp. As they marched past, the lieutenant colonel grew just a bit taller, his chest a little more puffed up, as he said to me in an aside, "Hell of fine troops." I asked him if he had many attempted escapes. He said no, but that if I went to a camp near the Mexican border, I could see the POWs light out "like striped-ass apes."

A tough German sergeant in one of the camps put us in a most precarious position. Having entered the camp and recorded a number of messages, the sergeant came to us in a very belligerent voice and said that this had to stop—it was treason. There were four of us in the midst of hundreds of German POWs, with the nearest armed United States troops in high watch towers at the corners of the camp. I acted instinctively, took the last glass disc we had recorded, broke it over my knee, and handed him the pieces. I repeated that no one was forced to send a message, that it was purely voluntary, and if he was speaking for the entire camp we would leave. The tension was broken, and we were relieved to get out of that camp!

Back in New York, our recordings were acknowledged as an exceptional propaganda coup. The messages—two or three at a time—were inserted into regular broadcasts of news and comment to Germany. Each broadcast indicated that messages from Hans or Rolf or Erich would be heard tomorrow at such and such a time. Some years later I had occasion to talk to Germans in Germany who told me how relieved they had been to hear from their loved ones. While I know of no scientific evaluation of these harmless messages in getting our news and views across, I believe they must have ranked very high in attracting and holding listeners.

The VOA grew. Its technical facilities were steadily improved and a relay broadcasting station was set up in London. It became known as ABSIE, the American Broadcasting Station in Europe. The fact did not escape German authorities that not only were American troops building up in England, but the Voice of America was now in Europe itself.

Early in 1944 (I believe it was February) I was asked to go to London to head the German broadcasting section of ABSIE. In the company of the French journalist, Pierre Lazareff, and a comical Russo-American producer, I landed at Prestwick. From there we traveled by train to wartime London. The blitz was over, but the V-1 and V-2 rockets were still to come. Although I was well acquainted with German air attacks on London, it was a shock to see the ruins—buildings totally destroyed and a shocked and tired people. The pubs were still serving ale and beer—not up to peace time standards perhaps, but they made pretty good sandwiches containing only fat meat.

As civilians in wartime London we had to find our own digs. With Henry Hatfield, my good friend of Columbia days, and Golo Mann, the second son of the famous German writer Thomas Mann, we located a flat in a basement in South Kensington. Many a night after work at ABSIE, which was located in the British Geaumont Building on Wardour Street, I had to walk through Hyde Park to our flat in South Kensington.

The work was exhilarating, particularly working with Golo Mann, a gifted writer who was to make his mark as a historian in postwar Germany. One of the most challenging things we did was to monitor the speeches of Joseph Goebbels, Hitler's vituperative propaganda minister, then analyze, dissect, and reply to Goebbels within a hour or so. Golo did the writing and then I went on the air as Alfred Zimmerman to read our reply.

There was an eerie lull in London when I arrived there. This was to be shattered shortly by the first V-1 rockets to hit London. The V-1s had a devastating effect on Londoners. The eerie noise they made as they approached the target, their cut-out, and the sharp whistle followed by the explosion of the house or factory they hit, left London nearly a deserted city.

Families with children had stayed out of town. On Sundays one could walk and find few people on the streets. Still the essential personnel—police, firemen, hotel employees, et cetera kept a stiff upper lip and performed their duties in an heroic fashion. While there may have been some black market activity, I was never aware of it. My admiration for the British was boundless. I saw many of them sleep in the dank, smelly tube stations, getting small provisions in little net bags. Morale was not high.

We did not suffer. We had access to the U.S. Army mess in Grosvenor House. We also had ration cards. Feeling rather guilty, we would splurge our entire month's meat ration on a great, good steak, which I cooked in our South Kensington flat. One morning a V-1 hit our little butcher shop. There was nothing left of it but a hole in the ground—and no more steaks!

We found the V-2s less devastating because you heard nothing until the explosion took place—and when you heard it, you knew you had survived. Still one longed to get out of London every once in a while. I recall two such outings.

Once was for a whole week to Harlech, Wales. I can still hear the silence of the place, broken not by rockets but by the humming of the bees. I was the only American there along with some thirty Englishmen on leave. They descended upon me and we had long discussions lasting well into the night. I recall their particular interest in our racial problems. I pointed out that they had their origins in the early slave ships that brought the black slaves to America, but that we were working on the problem. I noted that the British could not really fully understand the problem, since at that time they had no blacks in England. Not too many years later, however, they would experience racial disturbances after the Empire had fallen apart and West Indians started moving to England. One of the Brits I met there has remained a friend for life and we saw each other not long ago.

The second outing was brief, but had a comical twist to it. With two members of ABSIE I took a train to Henley-on-Thames one beautiful Sunday. As we walked into the town we decided to see whether we could rent some bicycles. A boy on a bicycle came along and we inquired where we might rent some. He told us to wait a bit and disappeared into a house, presumably his home. At this point two men who had been observing us sauntered over and politely asked if they could be of help. When we stated our desire to rent some bicycles, they asked us to follow them. They led us right straight into the police station. We were under arrest! A police officer interrogated us and after we had satisfied him that we were not German spies, he let us go. It appeared that a military exercise was in progress, during which some "German parachutists" were dropped into the countryside.

My work in German POW camps in England came to the attention of Edward R. Murrow. This marvelous man invited me to participate in his "This Is London" programs, which were widely heard in the United States during World War II. I marveled at the way in which he put his guests at ease, although I noticed that a constantly burning cigarette in his hand hid a tension throughout the rehearsal and broadcast. Ed Murrow asked CBS to notify my wife in New York when I would be on the air with him and she heard me. Although I did not see Ed Murrow often, I felt an immediate bond with the man, which became evident some years later.

Not all of our programs at ABSIE were just talk shows. We needed some music, and that was provided by Glenn Miller. This famous band leader, now a major in uniform, was directing a big band in England built around members of his peacetime band, but augmented by distinguished musicians from the Boston Pops and other musical organizations at home. I went to see Glenn Miller to ask him if he would do some records for us, which we would use in our broadcasts. He agreed.

In the next few days I taught Miller enough German phrases for him to carry on a brief dialogue with my secretary, a beautiful girl from Brno, Czechoslovakia, who acted as mistress of ceremonies. She spoke perfect German, of course, and Miller, his soloist Johnny Desmond, and others joined in the fun. We did the recording in a BBC studio somewhere in London. It was great fun to work with him and we all grieved at his disappearance shortly thereafter on a flight out of England.

London in 1944 was the abode of many famous people. I saw young King Peter (now an ex-king) of Yugoslavia, talking to another person on a street corner. The haughty French General Charles de Gaulle could often be seen walking in the city. The East Europeans were busy forming shadow governments in exile, which they hoped to transplant to the lands of their birth as soon as the war was over. And, of course, the doughty Winston Churchill could be seen entering and leaving No. 10 Downing Street, as could Anthony Eden and other British wartime figures. The American Embassy was headed by a moody New Englander, John Winant, who, some time later, took his own life. At that time virtually all official as well as unofficial Americans came to the embassy. Journalists by the score were poised for the invasion of

France, which everyone knew was coming, but only a very select few knew when.

When D-Day came on June 6, 1944 Allied planes covered the predawn skies over London. Forty-five years later I can still hear the roar of their engines as they flew toward the Channel and into Occupied France.

Broadcasting from ABSIE took on a different air now—an air of expectancy and nervous anticipation on when it would all end. Then came the liberation of Paris after the loss of many American, British and French, as well as German lives. Many of the journalists, broadcasters, et cetera, now moved out of London and to Paris. Plans were being made to bring ABSIE and the VOA to the continent.

I was given a breather in December of 1944 and allowed to go home. It was most gratifying to find out how well my little wife had coped with life in New York. We had a brief vacation in Williamsburg, Virginia, and saw some old friends in Charleston. But this was only a pleasant interlude.

Soon I was back on a plane to London first, then Paris, and finally Luxembourg, where we had established the first American radio station broadcasting in German on the continent. Since Luxembourg was still in a military zone, the head of the station was an American colonel, a Philadelphia lawyer. I was to serve as his deputy and executive officer.

For reasons never quite clear to me, the Philadelphia lawyer never seemed to like me. Our cooperation nearly came to an end when the Germans were finally defeated in May of 1945 and General Eisenhower wanted to address the defeated German nation. We had the advance copy of his speech. The Philadelphia lawyer informed me that he would read the German translation, which was what the Germans would hear. It was a tough decision I had to make—the colonel must not read the Eisenhower address in his Yiddish German. I informed him that Golo Mann, with his impeccable German should do it. The colonel yielded, but we were never friends thereafter. I had to strike down another idea spawned by him. He felt that our broadcasting diet should consist chiefly of readings from the Old Testament and music composed by Chopin. I could understand the rationale of his thinking, but felt we would soon have few, if any, listeners in Germany.

I had occasion, while stationed in Luxembourg, to make some field trips into Germany. I felt a curious sensation the first time I crossed into Germany, the land of my birth. In Frankfurt I looked for the Goethe house. There was nothing there but rubble. In Cologne I met Konrad Adenauer. I was not to talk to him again until he had retired as Chancellor of the Federal Republic of Germany during the last year of his long life.

The cities of Germany lay in ruins. In Wuerttemberg the houses were leveled and one could easily look over what was left of them. Everywhere people seemed on the move, going somewhere or nowhere. I saw young women on bicycles at a barrier put up by the MPs waiting to be cleared to pass. Only at the farm houses was there still the semblance of normality. I recall that I visited one such farm house, breaking the rule that there was to be no fraternization with the enemy, to exchange some coffee and tea for sausages and freshly baked bread. The farmers were fearful that they would be overrun by fellow Germans leaving the rubble of the cities and starvation behind them. Everywhere one saw a haunted look in the Germans' eyes. This was not to excuse what they had done, but it was only human, and I believed then that

America should help these people get back on their feet now that the war was over. Saddest of all were the young women and young mothers whose fathers' and husbands' whereabouts were unknown.

At one of the ever-present MP barriers near Stuttgart, we gave a ride to a winsome young German woman. When we dropped her off at her home, which she shared with her mother and a young daughter, she told us that she had little expectation of ever seeing her husband again since he had been taken prisoner on the Russian front.

Interestingly enough, when we crossed into Austria we found Austrian flags flying and no Nazi flags. Every Austrian in the Tyrol must have been in the Austrian underground, to hear them tell about it.

We spent some time in General Patton's domain. Everything was spit and polish. I was reminded by an MP that I should not remove my military cap when riding in a jeep. However, this charismatic American general was quite popular with his German subjects; perhaps he reminded them of Rommel or even Hindenburg.

On a late summer day in early September 1944, I set out in a jeep with three other officers from Radio Luxembourg for Frankfurt. Our mission: to establish the first station of a postwar German radio network on German soil. As we descended the Hunsrueck Mountains to the Rhine River, we saw a jeep coming in our direction. We weren't traveling over thirty five miles per hour, but before any of us knew it, the oncoming jeep got its right wheels off the pavement, cut too sharply trying to get back on, and came directly into our path. The driver of our jeep and two captains in the back seat were thrown clear as we hit the jeep broadside. Since I was sitting next to the driver, I was slammed against the dash and went down a twenty-five-foot embankment in the jeep. At first I felt no pain but knew I was bleeding from a cut above my right eye. When I tried to get up, however, my right leg refused to function. A jeep carrying two Frenchmen, one of whom claimed to be an "assistant docteur," examined me and found nothing amiss. He dressed the cut above my eye. Another jeep with Americans came along. The driver picked me up and drove me to Frankfurt, which was four hours of sheer torture since, as it turned out, I had fractured the *acetabulum* in my right hip—the socket that holds the hip joint. What made matters worse was that I had a residual cold, and every time I coughed, it hurt like blazes. When we arrived at the Ninety-seventh General Hospital in Bad Nauheim, a suburb of Frankfurt, the medics cut a hole on the side of the jeep to get me out. Mercifully a shot of morphine put me to sleep. When I awoke in the morning I heard the surgeon explain to the general in charge of broadcasting what the diagnosis was—that I would be hospitalized for some three months.

The experience in a military hospital was not totally uninteresting. The chief orthopedic surgeon discovered that I was a graduate of Oberlin College, the very college from which his wife had graduated. A communication with her confirmed that yes, indeed, she remembered me well. Dr. Urist, who later became a noted orthopedic surgeon on the West Coast, made me his unofficial assistant as soon as I was able to travel around the hospital in a wheel chair, reading X-rays and doing other little chores. There were some amusing incidents, too. One involved a soldier in a bed next to mine, who came in with two shattered knee caps. I noticed that on Sundays, when the commander of the hospital and chief surgeon came to inspect, my neighbor was unusually taciturn. I asked him

69

why and he told me that when he was brought in after the accident that had shattered his knee caps, he was given a local anesthetic. The operation was performed by some junior interns, with the doctor supervising shouting every so often, "No, no, not that way." The young soldier said, "How would you feel if your knees were operated on by a bunch of butchers?"

In December I was Z-eyed—shipped home on the *Queen Mary*, which was still a troop ship. Before I left the hospital, Dr. Urist gave me excellent advice on how to recover completely from my fracture. I followed his advice to the letter and, sure enough, my right hip never gave me any more trouble.

It was now 1945, the war in Europe was over as well as the war in the Far East. Fairfax and I retreated once more to Sandwich, Illinois. What to do? Go back to teaching, a field I had prepared myself for? What about the Voice of America? My worries ended when a letter arrived from the same little man who had introduced me to VOA in 1942, who was now a very important person in the VOA, inviting me to come back to the VOA as a kind of special assistant to him. I accepted with alacrity and we were back in New York City, again on West 110th Street, but in a more spacious apartment this time.

The immediate postwar years—indeed, the next eight years, 1945–53—that I spent at VOA proved to be difficult years. First, there was the question whether there would be a VOA at all. *Propaganda* was still a bad word as far as many Americans were concerned and Congress questioned the need for a propaganda organ in peacetime. But finally and grudgingly, Congress voted just enough money to keep us going. And second—what was the goal of the VOA going to be? What had been so clear and unifying during the long war—the destruction of Nazism and the defeat of the Germans—was now rather unclear. "Projection of America" became the slogan of the day, but what kind of America?

Was the VOA to reflect the real America, the good with the bad? Would the VOA report the news the way the *New York Times* or the BBC did? Yes, said many. Separate news from editorial comment and label the latter clearly as opinion.

Others felt equally strongly that such a course would present a picture of America consisting mainly of warts and no beauty spots. Didn't newspapers carry mainly bad news?

This divergence of views, growing ever sharper, led, in the first instance, to frequent changes at the top. The swing was from the soap to the ivy and back again. Gone were Elmer Davis and Robert Sherwood at the helm, and in came domestic radio directors and college presidents.

At the lower levels, many of the Americans who were happy to work at the VOA during the war sought more lucrative jobs at CBS, NBC, and Mutual. At the language desks, some of the wartime greats returned to their countries of birth now that Hitler was gone. All were aging, and many were completely out of touch with what was transpiring in Europe and Asia. The winds of change, which swept away not only Nazism and Fascism, but also old monarchies and prewar right-wing regimes, had not been felt by the refugees now living in an America that was settling into an uneasy peace.

Only one short year after the war had ended in Europe, Secretary of State Jimmy Byrnes made public for the first time, at the "highest United States government level," that indeed a great and ever-widening gulf was developing between our former Soviet allies and ourselves. Where we had envisioned coalition governments

71

of all hues, from right to left, the Soviets were determined to have only communist puppets in Eastern Europe. By 1948 they had achieved their objectives, with communist stooges in place in every one of the Eastern European states.

Then there was the question of defeated Germany. No one, not a single country that had been invaded by the Nazis, wanted to see the return of a powerful Germany. On the other hand, the division of Germany into four zones of occupation was not the permanent goal of the Western allies. While a dangerous Germany with a strong military force was forever to be prevented from once again emerging, a united Germany—perhaps neutral—carefully kept from becoming for the third time in this century a war-making machine, was the goal of the United States, the United Kingdom, and France. Berlin was scarcely thought of in those early postwar years as the Berlin we know today. Vienna was not envisioned as a four-power city nor Austria an occupied country for the next ten years.

All of these developments were reflected in the broadcasts of the VOA. There were those who felt that the Soviets were the enemy and would have to be fought at some future time. They lamented the fact that "Old Blood and Guts" Patton had not been allowed to drive on to Berlin; that Churchill had not had his way and the mission through Greece undertaken, keeping the Soviets out of Eastern Europe. Yalta for them become synonymous with treason.

Others felt equally strongly that the Soviets, with their losses of human lives in the millions had a point. Never again would they permit a warlike Germany to invade their lands. And those who held these views could justify the Soviet action in installing a communist buffer zone all along the Russian frontiers.

These conflicting views, held by many Americans outside of New York City or Washington, D.C., were bound to lead to some sort of clash. It came in the form of a junior senator from Wisconsin. Senator Joseph McCarthy, from the state that had produced the liberal Lafolette, stumbled into his almost obsessive anticommunist posture quite by accident. It is doubtful that he knew who Karl Marx was or what Lenin had espoused. It was sufficient for him to catch the prevailing winds of anticommunism and see communists under virtually every bed in the United States. His very first target was the Voice of America, a good choice from his and his young henchmen's point of view. Wasn't the Voice of America full of dangerous foreigners?

When lightning struck, I had risen to the position of program director of the VOA, one of the three top jobs under the director. This was a neat rise for a young teacher of German language, who worked only part time for the VOA at the beginning to the top level which a career person could expect at the VOA. My job did not concern policy-making, although I had the opportunity during our daily meetings with the policy-making people to put in my two cents worth. I was brash and young enough to do so. My job was to staff some forty language desks at the VOA and to see to it that programs were properly prepared and aired. I established the first Russian Desk at the VOA. I sought out career officers in the State Department for their views on who might be good at the Russian Desk, the Persian Desk, et cetera.

I had followed the unfortunate developments in Europe during the forties and early fifties with great misgivings. Having been reared in a small town in Illinois where there were only two Democrats out of two thousand souls, with the *Chicago Tribune* of General McCormick as the town's daily intellectual nourishment, I tended to be more conservative than liberal. Still, my Midwestern conservatism was leavened by my Oberlin College experience and my academic friends, most of whom tended to qualify as "liberals." I had voted for FDR each time except in 1940, when I thought the barefoot boy from Indiana, Wendell Wilkie, would keep us out of the war. I admired the little man from Missouri, Harry Truman, and particularly how he stood up to the Russians.

At the VOA I sought to steer a middle course between Scylla and Charybdis, calling on foreign service officers acquainted with the country and language to which they would be broadcasting to ride herd on the former refugees and their squabbles. I hired ardent anticommunists, like the Russian General Alexander Barmine, the first major Soviet defector, to head the Russian Desk. At the same time, I took on people who were known to hold "liberal" views, like the great wartime commentator, Raymond Swing. I had frequent disagreements with political directives that at times seemed to run counter to what I understood the administration's policies were. This led to some conflicts with the policy-setting people. It never occurred to me, however, that their views sprang from a belief in Communism.

Indeed, I found two communists in the VOA, more than Senator McCarthy ever found, and as far as I know, they were the only communists ever found working for the VOA. Both were Eastern Europeans, one a Pole, whose name I found after an article bearing his name was published by a Polish newspaper. When I fired him, he returned to Poland and a career as a communist journalist in Warsaw. The other was a Bulgarian, who, I discovered, was submitting VOA scripts in Bulgarian to the Bulgarian mission in Washington. I don't recall what happened to him after he was fired from the VOA.

When McCarthy struck in 1953, the VOA was without a leader. We had been fortunate in having as director of the VOA the highly capable and congenial foreign service officer, Foy D. Kohler of Toledo, Ohio. He was a Russian specialist, and although he had not previously had any radio experience, he learned fast. His standing in the foreign service earned him the respect of the professionals in the State Department. Under his aegis the VOA experienced a renaissance after the rather dismal early postwar years. Unfortunately, this able career officer, who had led the VOA in the early fifties, had left for reassignment in Washington. A radio man without gumption was brought in to head the VOA. When McCarthy began to decimate the VOA, the new director did not even appear at our policy meetings, explaining that he would outwait this "beneficial" purge and not be soiled by it. I startled him no end one day, when he used the words *Homo sapiens,* by telling him that McCarthy would misunderstand that expression.

I felt certain of my own position in the VOA. As a product of the Midwest, with no membership in any organization other than the scholarly Modern Language Association, I was generally known to have a fairly conservative outlook. I felt I had little to fear.

Then my wife in Leonia, New Jersey, where we had moved after the birth of our first child, received a call from Bobby Kennedy on Senator McCarthy's staff to report to the Waldorf Towers the next day.

When I got there, I saw to my dismay a little man, who was on my staff at the VOA, sitting behind a desk surrounded by steel filing cabinets containing few facts

75

but many rumors about VOA personnel. This little man, a stamp collector and a neighbor of mine in Leonia, who held a technical position, had apparently kept detailed notes about anything I said during our staff meetings. For example, a recommendation of mine to look at the Herb Bloc cartoon in the *Washington Post* lampooning McCarthy was considered subversive by him, et cetera, et cetera.

The session with Cohn and Shine, the "two gum-shoes" of the senator, was a bit unnerving—not that I feared for my own fate, but I knew that anything I said would be used against someone. It was well known, for instance, that I disputed, perhaps too vigorously, a Washington decision to cut back on Israeli broadcasts. I never thought that this decision was politically motivated and knew that it was a judgmental decision forced upon the VOA by a cut in the budget. Since the man, however, who had ordered the cutback was a target of the McCarthy gang for other reasons, my dispute with him was considered the action of a good guy against the bad guy.

And so it went. Did I know anything about communism? When a public affairs officer in London denied having read Karl Marx, he was castigated for being in a job that was supposed to fight Communism when he knew nothing about the enemy. When I allowed that I had read *Das Kapital,* an effort was made—unsuccessfully—to label me procommunist.

Among my good friends in the VOA was an ex-Austrian, who had generally thrived under my direction. I knew of his background and knew that he did not have any leftist leanings. He became one of the targets of the self-styled "loyal American underground," the terrorist organization in the VOA. I defended him and undoubtedly saved his skin. When the interrogation at the Wal-

76

dorf Towers was completed, I was told to report to the McCarthy Committee in Washington the following week.

There they sat around a long table, their names well known to me—Fulbright, Mundt, McClellan, et cetera. And then there was the chief interrogator himself, the man from Wisconsin. I stood my ground, and although I felt I had not allayed all suspicions about myself, or the VOA, I had at least earned the vocal respect of the conservative senator from South Dakota, Karl Mundt, who asked me to send him my views on what the VOA should do—whether it should be moved to Washington, D.C., and whether it should be integrated into the State Department.

I came out of that meeting with my skin barely intact. I was satisfied that I had saved several VOA employees, but was totally nauseated by the whole thing. I felt soiled because honest differences with others were interpreted as politically motivated rather than judgmental differences. McCarthy and his minions did not consider me a fit subject to be put on TV, for which I was grateful. I came out determined that I would leave the VOA and leave government service altogether.

In those early postwar years, there were also some very pleasant moments. Three of them were the births of my three children. When we were worried in the first years of our marriage that we might have a baby we could not afford, we were worried later that we could not have any children. But early in 1946 Fairfax, my wife, became pregnant, and in January of 1947, Ursula was born. She was the happiest event in my marriage so far. Her arrival led us to buy a small house—the price was $14,500—in Leonia, New Jersey. My wife and daughter spent much of the summer of 1948 in a farm house shared with the Hatfields in Kent, Connecticut. I made it up there from

77

New York every weekend, but always just by the skin of my teeth. It seemed that every Friday afternoon, when I wanted to make the last train to Kent, the director would call a meeting that I had to attend. However, he excused me when he learned what my predicament was. Those weekends with my wife, my young toddler, and our good friends were precious.

In 1949 we were blessed with a second beautiful daughter whom we named Fairfax, after her mother. And in 1951, a son, whom we named Frederic, was born.

Motherhood was not my wife's greatest joy. Indeed, while she was pregnant with Frederic in 1951, I took the eldest, Ursula, out to Sandwich, Illinois, to my mother, in order to ease the burden of taking care of a house, a baby daughter, and carrying an as yet unborn child.

Ursula spent an idyllic summer with her grandmother. Still, when the time came for me to pick her up, she leaped over a three- or four-foot fence into my arms. Our return to Leonia by car was not without danger. Ursula whiled the time away by catapulting from front seat to back and back again. On our first night out she finally got sick from overexcitement, but we made it home safely.

This was the time when the first rift occurred in our marriage. She is not here to explain her side of the story, or to dispute my version. I believe, in retrospect, that it was a combination of circumstances that contributed to the crumbling of our marriage. There had been nearly two years of absence from each other during the war. There was my complete absorption in my work at the VOA—my climbing the ladder to the top. And finally, there was the different attitude we had toward our three children. I am certain Fairfax loved them, but she had the burden of taking care of them, which I did not, and

it was difficult for her. The thought that I might termi-
nate the marriage flitted briefly through my mind, but
I rejected it and knew I would never divorce the mother
of my children as long as they were totally dependent on
their parents.

Let me back up a bit now. While Foy Kohler, future
U.S. ambassador to Moscow, was still the director of the
VOA, he asked me one day what plans I had for the
future. I had naturally thought about the future, since
I knew I was as high as I could go at the VOA, and I was
still in my thirties. He asked me if I had ever considered
the foreign service.

My experience with the foreign service had not been
exactly one to make me want to enter it. For one thing,
I wondered how a service allowed, indeed urged, its officers to come to New York and shop for jobs with the
VOA. My contacts with career officers in State led me to
believe that I scarcely fitted a service of cautious, careful
officers, devoid of almost any knowledge of administration, people who were quite elegant, but who pined to live
abroad and not at home in Washington. There were notable exceptions, of course, like Foy Kohler and, as I was
to discover, many others. However, I was action-oriented,
had a big job, did the hiring and firing, and supervised
nine hundred people. How could I fit into such a service?

When I mentioned my doubts about entry into the
foreign service, Kohler said that the service was changing
rapidly and there was need for men like me. He persuaded
me to try my hand at it via a very wise program called
Section 507, which allowed a trickle of capable and experienced civil service employees to enter the foreign
service after taking and passing examinations conducted
by experienced government officials. This was a far better
program than the later Wriston Program, which forced

virtually all State and USIA officers to make a choice to accept the foreign service or eventually lose their jobs. For many this turned out to be a disaster. Completely unqualified to live abroad—usually not linguistically trained—they frequently became the objects of scorn by the regular service.

I had another problem. I was program director of the VOA, a GS-15, the highest civil service grade then extant. Where would I start in the foreign service? When Kohler asked me what grade of the foreign service I would try for, I said FSO-1, the highest foreign service grade then existing. He smiled and said that he was not surprised, but warned me that it was most unlikely that I would be awarded the FSO-1 grade, and that I should be content with a lower grade.

On a sultry, hot day in June 1952, I took my exams in Washington, D.C. Perhaps it was my self-assurance, gained at the VOA in various responsible jobs; maybe it was my feeling of indifference on how the exam would come out. But I answered the questions with frankness. When asked by one of the examiners how I would negotiate a trade agreement in view of my stated lack of expertise in the economic field, I replied that in my experience with U.S. embassies I had always found at least one—and frequently more—economists on the staff. With their help and backing I thought I would be able to negotiate the agreement. Asked where Los Angeles got its water supply, I answered that I didn't have the faintest idea. Asked if I was ready to serve any place in the world, I replied in the affirmative, adding, however, that I would hope my linguistic accomplishments would be taken in account in assigning me. So it went.

In due time I was notified that I had passed the exams and that if I was still interested could become a foreign service officer, class 2, provided I was cleared by security and the medical department. I was happy to settle for class 2, since I saw no way to go any further in the VOA, and the idea of working abroad appealed to me. My mentor, Foy Kohler, congratulated me and assured me that I did the right thing.

But all of this happened before the McCarthy onslaught and his attack on the foreign service. I saw officers who had established solid reputations as objective political analysts drummed out of the service—the old China hands—and many others whose careers were blighted. And I noted that there was no one around to defend these men, not even the highly esteemed soldier-President Eisenhower; not the moralizing secretary of state John Foster Dulles, and least of all the McCarthyite security chief in the State Department. All this did not augur well for the future. I was sworn in as a foreign service officer, but remained for the nonce at the VOA.

Then came the McCarthy bloodbath.

Having survived, I was sick watching the spectacle of decent men and women harried and pilloried by the likes of Cohn and Schine. I decided I had had it with the United States Government.

I called my old friend—perhaps too strong a word—Ed Murrow, who was now unhappy as a vice-president at CBS. He saw me immediately. After some reminiscences about the London of 1944–45 that we both knew, I told him I was looking for a job. Looking me straight in the eye through the smoke of his ever-present cigarette, he said he would give me a job in television. I told him I knew nothing about television, to which he replied, "Neither does anyone else, but we're looking for people with ideas." Then he added ominously, "But if you're running from McCarthy, you have come to the wrong place—he's after me."

The day after my interview with Ed Murrow was a fateful day indeed. My mail contained notification that I was being assigned to the American Embassy in Vienna, Austria. Perhaps no other assignment could have kept me out of CBS and a career vastly different than the one I followed. When I called Ed Murrow to thank him for his kindness to me, and that my wife and I had opted to go to Vienna, he said he thought I had made the right decision, wished me well, and offered a lending hand in case I ever needed it.

My career of eleven years at the Voice of America was over.

# *Vienna*

## The Making of a Foreign Service Officer

Oɴ July 8, 1953, to the accompaniment of the well wishes of faithful co-workers at the VOA, we boarded the SS *Constitution* for our voyage to Europe. Flying the Atlantic was not yet a must for foreign service officers reporting to or leaving posts.

Our little family was five now, our children aged six, four, and two. Also aboard the ship was a brand-new green Studebaker, the model with the propeller nose. It was the only time in my life that I was happy to see the Statue of Liberty recede in the background as we entered the Atlantic. I was happy to leave, for a while at least, our unhappy McCarthy-riddled land. But I also embarked with some trepidation about my first assignment in the foreign service, and the reception I would be accorded by the professionals who had worked their way up the ladder from the bottom. How would they view this interloper, who, to be sure, had a reputation as a smart, can-do guy with a bigger job behind him than most would ever hold, and who knew the German language far better than most of them?

We landed in Genoa, Italy. I had never driven a car

in Europe before, didn't know Genoa, and didn't know my car had to have a *carnet* to cross borders. A kind vice consul met us at the port and loaded my family into his car, taking them to a hotel, while I waited for our car to be off-loaded. Once this was done I had to find my way to the hotel, where the vice consul had deposited my family.

Nothing daunted, we set out for Vienna via Switzerland the next day. I'll never forget all of the mountain passes in Switzerland, negotiating curve after curve with three small children who were sometimes well behaved and at other times rambunctious.

In Innsbruck in the Tyrol we stayed at a small airport motel-hotel, where the chef treated us to a marvelous *osso-bucco*. Our otherwise pleasant stay there was shattered somewhat when little Faxie, our four-year-old, got her fingers caught in a folding chair, ripping off a finger nail. Driving in the dark to the center of the city of Innsbruck with a screaming child beside me was an experience I'll never forget. But we got to Vienna, our nerves somewhat shaken by traveling through beautiful but unknown territory with three small children and crossing borders without a passport for the car. Once in Vienna, we were put up at the Bristol Hotel, the United States Army hotel. The British had the Sacher, the French La France, and the Soviets down the street from us had the Imperial and the Grand. Vienna was, of course, still under four-power occupation. This great city was divided into four sectors and "The Four Men in a Jeep" still sat on the sidewalk in front of Muehlhausen's toy store. There still were unpleasant incidents—and the Soviet Sector of Vienna was not the choice of most Americans. Many of the scenes in Orson Welles's classic movie, *The Third Man*, were still there in 1953.

Life in the Bristol, at a cost of fifty cents a day, was a pleasant experience. We had a *Kindermaedchen* almost immediately, and Fairfax and I were able to explore the restaurants, theaters, and museums during our free time.

My job was that of United States secretary in the Allied Commission. The Allied Commission for Austria received its mandate from the Control Agreement for Austria of June 28, 1946, signed by representatives of the four occupying powers. General Mark W. Clark signed for the United States.

The Control Agreement spelled out in fourteen brief articles the organization and mission of the Allied Commission for Austria. The Commission consisted of a top body, the Four-Power Allied Council, in which four high commissioners represented their countries, and an executive committee where the deputies of the four high commissioners represented their elements. Frequently the executive committee, acting on behalf of the Allied Council, could complete the necessary action required. Under the Allied Council and the executive committee functioned thirteen directorates, technical bodies dealing with various matters such as police, legal, finance, et cetera. Eight of these directorates matched one or more ministries of the Austrian government. The Vienna Inter-Allied Command was the arm of the Allied Commission for matters concerning Vienna as a whole.

The Allied Secretariat was established by the four powers in executive committee on September 27, 1945. It was an international secretariat, each element having a secretary and staff. The secretary of the element in the chair became the chief secretary. Thus I acted as chief secretary in January, May, and September; the British in February, June, October, et cetera.

The Secretariat was responsible for the preparation

of papers (highly standardized by the time I arrived on the scene), the correction of texts, preparation of agenda, issuance of official minutes, issuance of the *Allied Commission Gazette,* and transmittal of decisions and documents to the Austrian government. To this list of functions should be added the issuance of travel documents for persons wishing to traverse the four zones of Austria.

The principal mission of the Allied Commission for Austria was to "insure the enforcement in Austria of the provisions of the Declaration on the Defeat of Germany, to complete the separation of Austria from Germany, to assist the Austrian government in recreating a sound and democratic national life, to assist the freely elected government of Austria to assume as quickly as possible full control in Austria and finally, to insure the eradication of all traces of Nazi ideology."

Best remembered of the Control Agreement for Austria is Article 6a, which required written Allied Council approval of all Austrian constitutional laws, but which permitted "all other legislative measures and international agreements" to go into effect "if within 31 days of the time of receipt by the Allied Commission it has not informed the Austrian Government that it objects to a legislative measure or international agreement." This became the famous veto in reverse. It allowed the Austrian federal government to function, albeit with some limitations, especially in the Soviet Zone, as a central government making its own laws and appointing its own officials.

Meetings of the Allied Council took place every other Friday, twice a month. Executive committee meetings were held on the Fridays when the Allied Council did not meet. By the time I became secretary of the U.S. element in 1953, operations were fairly routine. Most of the staff work had been done by the directorates and put into proper form by the Allied Secretariat by the time actions went up to the Executive Committee or the Allied Council. In July of 1953, the distinguished American diplomat, Llewellyn E. Thompson, represented the United States; Sir Harold Caccia the British; the colorful Victor Hugo-esque Mr. Payart, France; and Mr. Ilychev, the Russians. Meetings took place in the "Haus der Industrie." Languages used were English, French and Russian. Ordinarily the agenda was approved, but under "Other Business" the Russians frequently raised subjects of a propaganda nature. I recall a special meeting of the Allied Council, in itself a rare procedure in the last years of the Allied Commission, called by the Soviet High Commissioner, to launch an attack against the United States for allegedly stationing United States troops in the French Zone of occupation.

A perusal of the *Gazette* for the years 1953 to 1955 shows that the subject matter acted upon by the Allied Council or the Executive Committee consisted of Austrian laws, Austrian relations with other countries and accession to international organizations, alleged Nazi literature and films found in Austria, and the appointment of Austrian officials.

A typical meeting during my time as U.S. secretary was that of September 1953. I was acting as chief secretary, it being a United States month. The Allied Council had no objections to the abolition of visas between Austria and Greece. It dispatched a letter to the Federal Chancellor of Austria, transferring to the Austrian government the right to issue passports to Austrian citizens, visas for entry into and exit from Austria to foreign nationals including Germans and Japanese, and made the Austrian government responsible for the political reliability of persons to whom entry and exit visas were issued. Each high commissioner reserved the right, however, to authorize entry to and exit from his zone of occupation. This same Allied Council meeting eased the surface movement within Austria of persons and goods, but again each high commissioner reserved his right to exercise control in his zone. The September 1953 meeting took note of a social insurance agreement Austria had reached with Germany and finally had no objection to some Austrian legislative measures.

At times the actions of the Allied Council or Executive Committee seemed rather picayune. For instance, in June of 1953 the Executive Committee approved a request from a Mrs. Maria Gremsl, living in Traenk-Toerl, British Zone, to have a telephone installed and have it connected to the switchboard at Moenichskirchen in the Soviet Zone. *Der Deutsche Soldaten Kalender* as well as a newspaper, the *Wochen-Echo*, and numerous German publications were banned. However, the Allied Council had no objection to the release of a film entitled *In Flagranti*.

Not all of the work of the Allied Commission was onerous. Since it was the supreme body in Austria, one of its functions was to receive chiefs of mission from countries with whom Austria had reestablished relations. Normally, countries friendly to the West held back their ambassadors until one of the Western elements was in the Chair, and friends of the Soviets waited until the Soviet high commissioner presided.

Not to be overlooked was the social side of the Allied Commission. The element in the Chair sponsored a reception after each meeting of the Allied Council. This allowed for some amicable and quiet conversation between East and West even during the coldest part of the cold war. I was told by my colleagues in the Allied Secretariat, who had been there much longer than I, that the quality of the food and the libation had declined somewhat in recent years!

Each element also presented a motion picture for the edification of the other elements during the month of its chairmanship. I can still see those fields of waving grain and peace-loving Russians tilling the soil. It must be said the membership of the Allied Commission maintained a facade of unity and comity even when statesmen of the West and East were hurling thunderbolts at each other.

My Russian counterpart was a genial man named Koptelow. He was not difficult to get along with, but one day the Austrian papers carried an account of Koptelow trying to kidnap an Austrian citizen by pushing him into a car. His efforts were foiled by the Viennese police. We never saw Koptelow again.

I enjoyed the weekly social sessions following each meeting of the Allied Commission and hosted by the element in the chair at the time. But I missed using my knowledge of the German language, since my job did not call for contact with the Austrians. At one of these weekly social sessions I was in a conversation with the number two man in the Russian Embassy, Kudriavtsev, a man who had been involved in espionage in Canada. He was a gifted linguist. The subject on everyone's tongue was the proposed visit of Emperor Haile Selassie to Vienna, which the Commission was permitting. Since this was the first time that royalty was to visit Austria—the first royal visit since the last Habsburg left Austria—the Viennese were ecstatic. I asked my Russian counterpart if he had ever been to Ethiopia. He said no, but his colleague, Timoschenko, who was in conversation with an American colleague of mine, had been stationed there.

By pure coincidence, this same colleague and I were traveling together to the embassy. I mentioned to him that I understood from Kudriavtsev that Timoschenko had been stationed in Ethiopia. He looked at me and said, that was funny, because Timoschenko denied to him that he had ever been there!

To look back and evaluate the role the Allied Commission played in Austria, I would like to quote one of its founders. Ware Adams, an American foreign service officer who served in Vienna at the beginning of the four-power occupation, from the fall of 1945 until the spring of 1947, wrote in an article in the *Foreign Service Journal* the following: "The Allied Council for Austria achieved a success that was unique among efforts to administer occupied areas jointly after the Second World War. Among all the postwar Allied Commissions, from Bulgaria, Rumania and Hungary, through Germany and Italy, around to Japan and Korea, the only one that turned out as planned, satisfactorily to all those concerned, was the one in Austria."

If the Austrian leaders had support in their efforts to maintain the integrity of their land, it came in large measure from the Allied Control Commission for Austria. While we were in a period of Cold War confrontation during the early fifties, the West and the East maintained a cordiality and a spirit of cooperation in Vienna that might have been difficult for an outsider to believe. While there were frequent and bitter disagreements in the meetings of the Allied Council and the Executive Committee, there was no threat to end the operations of the council, the Allied Secretariat functioned smoothly to present papers to the Allied Council and ironed out disputes before they reached the council. It was a professional job.

A colleague of mine, Martin F. Herz, one of the first men to enter Vienna in July 1945, writes in his introduction to his *Witnesses to the Beginnings of the Cold War:*

> The allied disagreements over Eastern Europe, Germany, Greece, and Iran, which became magnified during this period, certainly were also reflected in the attitudes of the occupying powers toward each other in Austria. On the other hand, I can find absolutely nothing in the record, or in my memory, that would suggest that the detonation of atomic bombs in Japan had any effect on events or attitudes in Vienna, whether Austrian, Russian, or American. Later, when Czechoslovakia was taken over and Berlin was blockaded, we the Western allies as well as the Austrians did change our basic attitude because we went through a brief period when we even doubted that an Austrian treaty would be desirable. Our position, as well as that of the USSR in Austria, thus was sometimes fluctuating. But on the whole our policy was sound in supporting the freely elected Austrian government and its claim to a viable national existence free from foreign interference.

Although the Austrian Treaty was signed on May 15, 1955, the Allied Commission continued to mark time until July 27, 1955. On that date, with Jim Penfield, in charge of the United States element in the chair, the Allied Commission dispatched a letter to Federal Chancellor Julius Raab containing the following resolution:

> In view of the fact that the State Treaty, reestablishing an independent and democratic Austria enters into force as of this date, the Control Agreement for Austria of 28 June 1946 ceases to be in

effect in conformity with Article 20 of this Treaty. Consequently, the Allied Council declares the termination of the activities of the Allied Commission for Austria.

The Allied Council, having fulfilled the tasks imposed upon it by the Control Agreement, expresses to the Austrian people and government its best wishes for a prosperous and happy future in freedom and peace.

My job during the last two years of the occupation of Austria and of the Allied Commission was not a job sought after by foreign service officers. It was a peripheral and obviously not a permanent job. Although nominally in the Political Section of the embassy, the holder of the job was not housed in the embassy of his country but rather in the Allied Commission Building on Schwarzenberg Platz. Indeed, my predecessor in the job was a former military officer, now a civilian, who was clinging to a job with the foreign service by his fingernails. Having recently reigned over a staff of nine hundred at the VOA, I now had a young FSO assistant and a secretary.

But I had great good luck. At the helm of our embassy in Vienna was a remarkable diplomat, a career Russian language officer, a Soviet specialist—in his first job as United States ambassador—but whom we called "High Commissioner" during the life of the Allied Commission. He was Llewellyn E. Thompson, a Coloradoan, with his charming wife Jane.

Thompson knew my background and treated me as though I had been in the service all along. Indeed, one day he asked me whether he should wear black or gray gloves on a certain occasion. I almost blurted out, "Mr. Ambassador, you have been at this a lot longer than I."

Instead I answered, "Gray." I could feel the warmth and good feeling this shy, quiet man showed me. It was this relationship that launched me on a successful foreign service career. Ambassador Thompson soon found out that I could be highly useful to him, and in a relatively short time he asked me to accompany him to his meetings with the Austrian chancellor and foreign minister, neither of whom spoke English. Frequently he would ask me to return to the chancellor or foreign minister for a clarification of their remarks. And I prepared the telegrams for his signature, which covered the meetings with the Austrians. Thanks to my fluent knowledge of German and my position as United States Secretary in the Allied Council, I was in regular and frequently daily contact with him. When we first met, he was neither optimistic nor pessimistic regarding the chances of an Austrian Treaty. With patience and quiet diplomacy he kept the lines to his Soviet counterparts open. He enjoyed the respect of his British and French colleagues. It was as his notetaker and interpreter that I became acquainted with the Austrian leaders. Ambassador Thompson had the trust of men like Figl, Schaerf, Raab and others of equal stature. After the treaty was finally signed Chancellor Raab called me to his office, telling me he had a special request. He wanted to know if his selection of a going-away present for Ambassador Thompson—he had just been assigned as United States Ambasador to Moscow—would please the ambassador. He led me through the narrow corridors of the *Ballhausplatz* to a room in which he had a painting of the signing of the Austrian State Treaty. I assured him that the ambassador would indeed be gratified by his gift—and so he was.

But I am ahead of my story. Neither Ambassador Thompson nor any members of the American Embassy staff in Vienna had reason to be optimistic about a resolution of the Austrian problem, in view of the hundreds of unsuccessful meetings that had been held since the end of World War II in 1945. Indeed, the emergence of the Federal Republic of Germany, its role in NATO, and the concomitant raising of tensions, made an Austrian Treaty appear to be more distant than ever.

In fact, in late 1954 and early 1955, if memory serves, we had some apprehension about the future of Austria. The Soviet high commissioner launched an attack against the United States for allegedly stationing United States troops in the French Zone of Occupation. There was concern voiced in some quarters that Austria might indeed suffer the same fate as Germany—that it might be divided, with Eastern Austria becoming a part of the Soviet Eastern European satellites. To most of us at that time it appeared unlikely that such a division would take place, for very little would have been gained by those undertaking such a process.

When the Austrian leaders were invited to Moscow to be told that the Soviets were now prepared to give their assent to a treaty, the process of completing it still took many hours of hard bargaining. I should point out that before going to Moscow, the Austrian leadership caused some concern in our embassy also—a fear that they might lose their shirts. As we know, that did not happen.

The days and weeks spent in hammering out the treaty in Vienna were exciting indeed. Ambassador Thompson generally met with his British and French colleagues in the mornings, and afternoons were given over to meetings of the four powers. In retrospect, it appears as incredible that Austria was not represented in these meetings. However, they were kept well informed.

When the last "t" had been crossed and the treaty was ready for signature, a weary Ambassador Thompson and staff relaxed, aware of the fact that we had participated in an event of importance in world history.

What brought about the Austrian State Treaty in 1955, or put another way, what caused the Soviets to agree to a treaty for Austria in 1955, can, of course, be answered with certainty only by the Russians themselves. Whether it was the fact that the Soviet Zone of Occupation in Austria was not comparable in importance to East Germany, whether it was realization that Austria after ten years was not likely to become a communist state, whether a policy of neutrality as pledged by the Austrian government had appeal to the Soviets, both because it would keep Austria out of NATO and a German sphere of influence, or because it might serve as inducement to Germany to follow suit, or whether the economic gains obtained from occupying Eastern Austria had after a period of ten years begun to decline, or whether Austria's independence would sever the northern and southern flanks of NATO—these are the reasons that have been advanced for a change in the Soviet position on the Austrian State Treaty. Whatever motivated this change, it pleased us. The terms of the treaty were viewed by the United States in light of whether they helped to keep Austria a viable, independent state or not. And it was over this aspect that the toughest bargaining took place.

A word about neutrality and Austria. In the world of the eighties, with superpowers, East and West blocs, and a so-called Third World (I say so-called because some members of that Third World or neutrals obviously cannot qualify as neutrals), the concept of true neutrality is totally acceptable to the United States. However, in 1955, many of my countrymen viewed neutralization as an alien concept: he who is not for us is against us. Fortunately, our statesmen of the time were farsighted enough not to succumb to the notion that a pledge of Austrian neutrality was a move against us.

When a representative of the Austrian embassy in Washington asked me in March of 1980 whether I would be willing to participate in a symposium on the Austrian State Treaty twenty-five years after the signing, I replied that I would deem it a great honor indeed to accept such an invitation. Although my service on behalf of the government of the United States spanned a period of over 31 years, and although I was fortunate to serve my country in various countries in crucial times, my association with Austrian affairs from 1953–57 remains, in retrospect, a high point of my entire diplomatic career, even though it came very early in that career.

I do not pretend that what I am about to say regarding the Austrian State Treaty is a work of scholarship. There are many, including American colleagues of mine, who have put into print the history of Austria from 1945 to 1955—the ten years of occupation of Austria by the four powers—and the efforts to redeem the pledge made in the Moscow Declaration of 1943 to treat Austria "as the first free country to fall a victim of Hitlerite aggression."

I should begin by saying that in my view—and this is shared by colleagues who at one time or another worked on some phase of an Austrian state treaty from 1945–55—that Austria owes its State Treaty above all to its own statesmen of the period. One could begin with Chancellor Karl Renner, the venerable first postwar chancellor of Austria, and go right down the line to the great statesmen (whom it was my great privilege to know) during the last two years of the occupation: Leopold Figl,

Julius Raab, Adolf Schaerf, Theodor Koerner, Bruno Kreisky, Oskar Helmer, and on and on. Each of them has earned a niche in the Austrian pantheon of heroes. For it was these men who trod a path strewn with risks and dangers through the field occupied by the four Allied powers of World War II. The job of holding together a war-torn Austria that was divided into four zones, with a capital also divided into sectors, was a task that can only be described as heroic. Lesser men than the Austrian statesmen of that time would have failed and Austria might have ended up as a divided country with no viability. Instead of an Austrian Treaty, there well could have been a German solution. It is a real tribute to these Austrian statesmen that the Cold War never became as cold—or as hot, if you like—in Austria as it did elsewhere.

The intervening years have happily seen Austria strengthen its position among nations, developing the concept of neutrality with the benefit of good relations with nearly all nations, and an economy that is flourishing. To see Vienna and Austria today is to make this American, *me*, proud to have participated, albeit in a minor way, in the events that brought this about.

With the Austrian State Treaty signed on May 15, 1955, the Allied Commission for Austria ceased to exist and the Palais housing its secretariat was turned back to the Viennese authorities. And with this event my job came to an end. I recall telling my wife early in 1955 to prepare for a move—to where, I didn't know.

But the ambassador had other ideas. He called me in and asked me to stay on as his political counselor, the third-ranking post in the Embassy. I was overjoyed. This was a job in the direct chain of command. I moved into the embassy, and my family and I into the splendid political counselor's house.

97

Our social life in Vienna left little to be desired. We made many good friends among the Viennese, some of whom have remained friends to this day. We entertained modestly but tastefully. The famous Vienna Opera performed nightly at the Theater an der Wien, the temporary home of this famous institution until the Opera on the Ring was restored upon the signing of the treaty. Seats were easy to come by. One could get two in the first ten rows for one hundred shillings, the equivalent of four dollars. We attended the opera at least once a week, and at the end of my tour in Vienna had probably seen and heard their entire repertoire. Theaters were going full blast, but while I could follow the German text easily, my wife could not. I performed a labor of love. On five consecutive nights I translated Schiller's *William Tell* for her so she might enjoy the performance of that old classic. Restaurants were aplenty and we patronized many of them.

The children were in the care of a wonderful old lady who took them everywhere and taught them German as spoken in Austria's capital. As long as the occupation lasted, they could attend the American military school.

When the United States military left, we had to find a school—Austrian schools were in ruins and overcrowded. Vienna was still in shambles—houses lacked repair and paint, yards and parks were unkempt. I was the ambassador's choice to help found an international school in Vienna. Together with British and Indian colleagues, we located a building, hired a British schoolmaster, established fees, and set up the curriculum and conditions for attendance. It was a major undertaking and many a night we wrestled with problem after problem: could the schoolmaster use corporal punishment (the result was negative); should every member of the embassy, with or without children, be assessed to keep the school going? There was considerable objection to this from the young officers who had no children. But we muddled through, and today, more than thirty years later, the American International School in Vienna serves not only families stationed in Vienna but those working in Eastern European countries as well.

The children loved Vienna. I taught Ursula, the oldest, to ride her first bicycle. We rode along the Canal, and were even stopped one time by a Viennese gendarme, who told us we were violating a Vienna ordinance by not dismounting at a certain place. To his question, "Didn't I see the sign to dismount?" I replied in perfect German that I had not. He then asked if I was Viennese—something about my accent no doubt—and I told him no. Further probing told him we were Americans, leading to his excusing us because undoubtedly some Viennese in front of us had not dismounted and we were then led astray—a fine Viennese bow to America!

And there was time to become acquainted with Austria. As I said earlier, I had a lot of time on my hands at the Allied Commission building, and no one in the embassy cared whether I was there or not as long as I performed my duties in connection with the ambassador's or his deputy's appearance at the weekly high commission meetings. So I took my wife and my car and visited the Austria outside of Vienna. We traversed the length and breadth of this small country; from Salzburg to the Woerther See; from Burgenland and Carinthia to the Tyrol and Vorarlberg, stopping at little inns, talking to the local people in pubs, reading local newspapers, and attending fairs and markets in Graz and Innsbruck and Eisenstadt. Some time later I astonished the Austrian chancellor when I mentioned a tiny village in Styria. He asked me how I came to know this little spot, hardly noticeable on the map, and I told him we had spent a night there. The Austrians were not slow in seeing that I knew their country and their language, a fact which stood me in good stead when I became political counselor of the embassy in 1955.

There was one alarming aspect to our stay in Vienna. It appeared to me that the slight rift in our marriage, which I felt before going there, was widening. We had some quarrels on our trips. I entertained thoughts of divorce, but knew as long as the children were young that would not happen.

Austria, in the two years of the post-occupation years that I spent there, was like a child that had been abandoned. True enough, Austria had maintained pressure on the occupying powers to get her freedom, but once obtained, felt lonely once the four flags came down from over the Allied Commission building and the occupying troops left for home. Where before the treaty was signed Austria had been a subject for discussion in at least 350 sessions, and the rest of the world knew about Austria's situation, after the May 15, 1955 treaty, Austria became a little country of seven million people with no role to play in world affairs.

I enjoyed my work as political counselor in the embassy. I was a steady companion to Ambassador Llewellyn E. Thompson on his visits to the Austrian chancellor and foreign minister. I prepared or supervised the preparation of the reports that went from the embassy to the State Department.

We had, of course, many visitors. Even while the occupation was still on, some congressmen ventured behind the Iron Curtain and traveled to Vienna, nearly one hundred miles into the Soviet Zone of occupation.

One such visitor was a Democratic congressman from North Carolina. At a reception for him he was particularly obnoxious, putting a rubber snake down ladies' bosoms and performing other similar coarse antics. He cornered me and asked me what would happen if the Russians suddenly closed the corridor from Salzburg to Vienna, our entry to the capital. I told him that we would all be in the same boat—prisoners in the city of Vienna. He reminded me, which was scarcely necessary, that he was a Democratic congressman from North Carolina and it would be our duty to get him out of Vienna to the nearest border. In exasperation I said we would do that, and in answer to his question on where he would be, I replied, "Communist Hungary!"

Another visitor to Vienna in those days was Sherman Adams, aide and confidante of President Eisenhower. He came on a weekend. The ambassador received him and then wisely went fishing, turning Adams over to me with the comment that I could show Mr. Adams Vienna better than anyone else. I spent that entire weekend escorting Mr. Adams and his party around Vienna, ending on a beautiful night at the restaurant on the Kahlenberg, the last of the Alps. We dined where we could see the lights showing Vienna at its best, and listened to Strauss waltzes emanating from the orchestra. I recommended the menu and Mr. Adams was pleased. When the bill came, Sherman Adams said he wished to pay his share of the bill! (I paid my share, which was not reimbursed by the United States Government!)

Probably the most dramatic event of my last two years in Vienna was the revolution in neighboring Hungary in October of 1956. The signing of the Austrian State Treaty a little more than a year before gave hope that the Cold War, which had raged for nearly ten years after the end of World War II, would abate. Some optimists even saw the possibility of a German treaty that would end that country's occupation and division. Those hopes were dashed when the students in Budapest, joined by workers and the militia, rose against their communist masters and were fired upon by the Hungarian police. What had started as a student uprising became a national revolt, the Soviet troops in Budapest withdrew, the borders with Austria were open, and the Hungarians had achieved a near miracle. They were free!

In our embassy in Vienna we followed the exciting events in Hungary with hope but with great trepidation. Was it conceivable that the Russians would allow Hungary to leave the Russian Empire and thus point to others—Poland and Czechoslovakia, for example—the way to freedom? Ambassador Thompson was highly sceptical and so informed the United States government.

But for twelve heady days, Austrians were crossing the border to visit old friends in Hungary, and Hungarians saw what Austria looked like. We had just parted with Mr. Wailes, who had been nominated to become minister in Budapest. He got there but never presented his credentials—and Budapest was to remain without an American ambassador for some years.

When the Russians struck with tanks and troops on November 4, 1956, thousands of Hungarian men and women died. There were estimates that as many as thirty thousand were killed. More than a quarter of a million Hungarians fled their country into neighboring Austria. On a Saturday afternoon a sizeable group—several hundred—Hungarian refugees came to the American embassy, demanding guns. I had the weekend duty and had little time to alert the ambassador. With an officer who spoke Hungarian I went out through the front door and spoke to the desperate refugees, telling them that we sympathized with them and their demands, but that we had no guns in the embassy. I told them I would pass on their views to Washington and somehow managed to calm them down sufficiently to leave the embassy. It was a slightly unnerving experience.

We established soup kitchens in Vienna. The wives of embassy officers worked day and night to get supplies and see to it that the bare necessities for the refugees were taken care of. But a long-time solution was necessary and indeed demanded by the Austrians.

This brought the vice-president of the U.S. to the scene. President Eisenhower dispatched Richard Nixon to Austria to assure the Austrians that we would help them with the two hundred fifty thousand Hungarians in their midst by taking a large number of them as emigres to America and finding other countries willing to take the rest.

Richard Nixon arrived on December 19, 1956. Ambassador Thompson assigned me as escort officer and handyman to Nixon. I was not too happy with the assignment. In my mind Nixon's name was associated with the McCarthy wing of the Republican party and my memories of McCarthy witchhunts were still very vivid.

I spent the next seventy-two hours—most of them awake—with the vice-president. I found him to be very different from the picture I had formed of him. He was a good listener, asked for advice and questioned it if he had any doubts, and worked hard and treated his Austrian hosts with respect and kindness. In fact, the Austrian press, particularly the organs of the Socialist party who had railed at his coming and had revived the Alger Hiss case and Nixon's alleged association with Senator

McCarthy, changed their minds about the man during the course of his visit.

Nixon saw everyone we thought he ought to see. Indeed, his routine was so strenuous that the ambassador—never physically a strong man—found it difficult to keep up with him. I recall one early morning when Nixon was already seeing the head of the International Red Cross that I missed Ambassador Thompson. I inquired of his butler where he was, since we were shortly to call on the chancellor. He told me he was still asleep, and I suggested he wake him. He said he couldn't do that, so with some trepidation I went to his bedroom, tapped him on the shoulder, and said that the vice-president was already downstairs. He woke with a start, shaved and dressed with lightning speed, and was quite ready when we had to leave to talk to Chancellor Raab.

On the last day of his stay in Austria, Vice-President Nixon had accepted an invitation from the governor of Burgenland to attend a luncheon. This easternmost province of Austria, part of which had belonged to Hungary prior to World War I, lay in the path of the fleeing Hungarians. The governor, a man named Wagner, was a tough, gruff Austrian, who had kept the police of his province from being infiltrated by Soviet-supported communists. I had told Nixon all of this.

On the way to Eisenstadt, the capital of Burgenland, Nixon asked me if I would translate for him at the luncheon. I told him that I would be happy to, but that I wasn't an official interpreter. I asked if he had a text of his intended remarks, and if so, it would be most helpful if he would let me scan it. He did and promptly fell asleep in the car. I found nothing very difficult to translate.

Upon our arrival in Eisenstadt, the governor and other ranking officials took the vice-president and his entourage to the beautiful Palais, where in an earlier age, Papa Joseph Haydn had conducted his symphony orchestra. Here Governor Wagner treated his distinguished guest to a beautiful luncheon laid out on tables set end to end with approximately one hundred guests, all of whom were men.

With the luncheon nearly over, Governor Wagner rose and delivered a rousing, anticommunist speech. Since I knew I would have to report his remarks to Washington, I sat directly opposite him and took copious notes. Nonetheless, I was just a bit taken aback when the governor, addressing me, asked me to tell the vice-president what he had just said. I did so since it was no great task to render his remarks into English. There was applause.

Vice President Nixon, sitting to the right of the governor, then stood up, and having seen the governor of a remote Eastern European province deliver a speech without a note in front of him, spoke without his script and gave a very different speech from the one I had read in the car.

Using every scrap of paper and paper napkins handed me by my neighbors, and sweating profusely, I scribbled as much of his remarks as I could. When he finished, I got up and gave what I would regard as a fair, if not word-for-word translation of his response to Wagner's toast.

After the applause had subsided, Governor Wagner rose once more. He knew me because some months earlier I had handed him an invitation from the U.S. government to visit the United States, in recognition of his staunch anticommunist stand under Soviet occupation.

He asked for quiet and then spoke briefly of his trip to America, telling his audience how much he had appreciated his stay there, and concluded with the remark:

"Gentlemen, I also learned a little English on my trip to America, and I can tell you that you have heard three eloquent speeches here, and in my view the last (my translation of Vice-President Nixon's) was the best."

The vice-president looked at me questioningly. I rose and explained that Governor Wagner wished to thank him for the trip to America. He concluded by thanking me for the translation. Every time I had occasion to see Richard Nixon in the years to come, I wondered if anyone ever told him what the governor had really said.

The Hungarian revolution of 1956 was the subject of great speculation in our embassy and by the Austrians. It was clear that a US military invasion to prevent the Soviets from returning was out of the question. For one thing, it would have violated Austrian neutrality, which we had vowed to uphold by signing the Austrian State Treaty. Would the Soviets have allowed the Hungarians to leave the fold if we had shown a threat of force? One has to remember that at that time we had the atom bomb and the Soviets did not. Could the Soviets have allowed the defection of one of its satellites? If so, Eastern Europe today would be quite different, and present spectacular changes in Eastern Europe would not have taken place.

Unfortunately nothing was done to help the Hungarians when a voice on the radio from Budapest cried for help. We did not even urge the secretary general of the United Nations to fly to Budapest. Unfortunately, our Western friends, Great Britain and France, had joined Israel in an invasion of Egypt without our prior knowledge. This doomed expedition confused the whole issue of Hungary. The attention of the world was diverted to another spectacle. But doubts were never resolved that if we had acted quickly and more menacingly than we had, we *might* have changed the course of history. When more than a decade later, I was to serve as United States ambassador to Hungary, men and women over fifty often rebuked me, as the representative of the United States, for our failure to act in their time of crisis. It was the only rebuke I ever had in Budapest.

Not all of our many visitors were as successful in their mission to Vienna as had been Richard Nixon. One of these was Scott McLeod, a protege of Senator Styles Bridges and now the security chief in the Dulles State Department.

At a reception for him on the patio and in the lovely garden of the embassy, McLeod, for whom I had been doing the translating, met the socialist minister of the Austrian government, Oskar Helmer. Helmer took McLeod to task, told him that his friend, Senator McCarthy, knew nothing about communism, and was indeed helping communism by his clumsy attacks on innocent people. McLeod, taken aback by this frontal assault, denied that he was a friend or henchman of McCarthy.

The dialogue found its way into one of the columns—I believe Drew Pearson's—where this incident was reported with great glee. I received a letter from McLeod in which he accused me of leaking the dialogue to the columnist, and left a not-so-veiled threat to my career. I denied the suggestion—quite truthfully—and heard no more of the incident.

Another visitor to Vienna was the twice-defeated Democratic candidate for the presidency, Adlai Stevenson. He came in August of 1956, a month during which most Austrian officials were on vacation. So was our ambassador. The chargé, an inexperienced officer with a rich UN background, wished to entertain Stevenson at his home and asked me to get Chancellor Raab and Foreign Minister Leopold Figl to come and meet Adlai. Thanks in part to the fact that there was a Polish reception that night, to which literally everyone went since Poland had just gained a new, more liberal government and had thrown off many of the severest restrictions, and thanks to Stevenson himself, who was held in high regard by the Austrians, they came.

Figl was in his cups. He greeted Stevenson by embracing him and calling him by first name—although they had never met. Stevenson was weary (he was on a return trip from Africa) and Chancellor Raab was taciturn and grumpy. The evening was dominated by the effusive Poldi Figl.

After all the guests had left, the chargé and his wife asked us to stay on for a nightcap. Having picked up our overcoats, my wife and I left. It was a cool night so we strolled leisurely to our house. Shortly after 6 A.M. the telephone by our bedside awakened me and I heard an anxious female voice telling me that the chancellor of Austria was missing his top coat and thought maybe I had picked it up. I told her that I would check at once, and that if I did indeed have his coat, would return it to him. She said the chancellor was already on his way and was having chills because he had no top coat. As I went down the stairs to find out if I indeed had his coat, I saw the black chauffeured car bearing Chancellor Raab drive up to our door. I had in fact taken the only remaining coat in the chargé's house. Who had taken mine I never found out. The thought of strolling down Vienna's streets after midnight, wearing the Austrian chancellor's only top coat was indelibly imprinted in my memory. And I never even checked the pockets!

Like all good things, my Vienna tour had to come to an end after a little over four years. It was preceded by the departure of Llewellyn Thompson to become ambassador to Moscow where he was to serve as a distinguished ambassador twice.

Although a few intimates called him Tommy, to me he was always Mr. Ambassador, until many years later in Washington, when I finally forced myself to call him Tommy. I owe so much to him. I learned patience from him, how to draw up maximum requirements, minimum ones, and when to compromise. Above all I learned how a diplomat develops trust and confidence in himself and from allies as well as adversaries. I saw him use the little step by step negotiation, moving a little forward with each step. He was the soul of discretion. And behind that usually solemn mien was a warm heart—something I always felt in his presence.

Before he left, he wrote two letters on my behalf—one to the assistant secretary of state for European Affairs, recommending me for a job in the European Bureau of the State Department, the other to the new U.S. ambassador to Bonn calling me to his attention. Both replied courteously but neither gave me a job. I had passed the test with Ambassador Thompson, but not with a lot of the old-timers.

My next assignment was deputy director of the Office of International Administration (OIA) in the Bureau of International Organizations. I had never heard of it. Ambassador Thompson said quietly: "You'll get known in Washington. Never mind the particular job."

Looking back, I have fond memories of my first assignment abroad as a foreign service officer. My association with Ambassador Thompson, the training I received, my relationship with the Austrian government officials which perhaps was closer than anyone else's in our embassy, are moments I will always cherish. I treasure the trips through Austria, from Burgenland to Vorarlberg and from Salzburg to Carinthia and Styria. I also had ample opportunity to become acquainted with Austria's Western neighbors—Italy, Switzerland, Germany, and yes, even Czechoslovakia. I still think back fondly of the operas in Vienna—the *Oper* and the musical comedies at the *Volksoper*. The *Burgtheater,* as well as other theaters in Vienna, provided us a rich fare with its fine actors and actresses. If the Voice of America gave me the opportunity to run a big show, the Vienna years taught me the art of negotiation as practiced by masters. My family thrived on the Austrian experience. I was ready now for greater tasks.

# Washington—the State Department, 1957–62

**W**E traveled home on the beautiful liner, the SS *United States*. There was no assigned seating the first night, but when our family of five sat down at one of the tables, the maître d' said, "Who told you you could sit there?" We learned the party was over.

Although I had been in Washington numerous times, we had never lived there. So house-hunting was the first order of business. We located a comfortable house on a rise in Bethesda, Maryland, just off River Road, then still a lovely two-lane road. This was to be our home for the next five years. The children were installed in good public schools and we settled into suburban living.

The job to which I was assigned was worse than I had anticipated. I have spoken in the past about peripheral and line jobs. This assignment was so peripheral that we were housed in offices above a garage in Virginia that was far removed from the State Department. Indeed, one of the hardships we suffered there were the ice-cold floors above the garage, which were open to the winds of winter. The temperature at desk level was ten to fifteen degrees warmer than on the floor. We found this out by actual tests we conducted with a thermometer!

The task of the Office of International Administration (OIA) was to prepare and defend a budget for United States' participation in international organizations—the United Nations, the entire family of the UN—UNESCO, ILO, WHO, et cetera. Since the United States, at this time, was contributing at least a third of the budget of these multilateral organizations, and much more to special funds outside of the regular budgets, this involved preparation and presentation of position papers to the U.S. Congress for the funding of large budgets.

U.S. personnel for these organizations also came into the purview of OIA, but since the U.S. had taken the position that American personnel working in the Secretariat of the UN and the others were international servants hired by the international organizations themselves, there was little input the OIA could make. It took the U.S. some time to realize that not everybody was willing to play by such rules. Consequently, other countries, particularly the Soviets, placed carefully vetted persons in key slots, whereas we could not count even on U.S. personnel in the Secretariat, many of whom did not share the views of the U.S. administration.

My immediate chief was a fine civil servant greatly devoted to the concept of multilateral diplomacy. Indeed, some years later he became a deputy director of UNESCO.

The Bureau of International Organizations (IO), of which the OIA was but one office—the other offices having to do with political support and guidance to our delegations to the UN family of nations, another with economic matters pertaining to multilateral affairs—and one in charge of arranging and financing meetings of international organizations.

Heading the bureau was another fine civil servant, Francis Wilcox, a scholarly, astute bureaucrat who knew his way around Washington. He had two deputies. One was a senior FSO who could scarcely wait to get back into the field. The other was a young and able political appointee.

My visits to the meetings of the United Nations, both the Security Council and the General Assembly, deepened my conviction that while the UN undoubtedly represented a noble concept, and that we were probably better off with it than without it, I thought early on in my stint as deputy director of OIA that we were paying too much for the privilege, and that others should pay a bit more for maligning the U.S. I felt particularly strongly about UNESCO, when I was told by a participant from another country, "You furnish the dollars, we have the ideas." I learned quickly that the annual assemblies of these organizations spent far more time arguing whether Communist China should be admitted and Nationalist China thrown out of the U.N. than the matters with which they were charged. I recall a General Assembly of the World Health Organization when a lot more time was spent on that issue than on the eradication of malaria. It was not that there weren't many good, conscientious international civil servants who were anxious to make the world a better place to live in, but most of them felt that the U.S. should supply the money to bring that about.

One of the organizations that I hoped would succeed was the International Atomic Energy Agency, the IAEA, headquartered in Vienna. But it, too, could only reflect the schism that existed between East and West.

Perhaps the worst aspect of my assignment to OIA was that I really did not have enough to do to keep me busy. We were amply staffed, chiefly by civil servants who knew the ropes, and I had time on my hands. Indeed,

I used to go to a nearby People's drugstore in Rosslyn, Virginia, to pass two or three hours over a small lunch by reading the magazines for sale there.

Just as woodworking helped to get me through the agony and inanity of the McCarthy years, it was brick-laying that kept me sane during the OIA days. I studied the art, bought bricks and concrete mix, found houses that were being razed, got the discarded bricks and went to work. I built an entire wall around a part of our garden in Bethesda as well as retaining walls near the garage. I was amazed at the strength my little wife exhibited in mixing concrete.

When the assistant secretary of the Bureau of International Organizations asked me one day to come to his office for a Saturday meeting, I assured him I would, but added that that would leave even less work for me for the rest of the week. He was somewhat dismayed by this—no bureaucrat would ever admit that he didn't have enough to do! The result of this was one I did not really welcome. He made my immediate chief, the director of OIA, a special assistant to him, and elevated me to the post of director of the OIA. I now had a better-sounding title but no more work than before.

This was the time when foreign service inspectors still inspected FSOs serving in the State Department and not only the FSOs in the field. We had such an inspection in the OIA. Two senior FSOs conducted hearings, interviewed a few FSOs in OIA and wrote their reports. I was very candid with them and told them about the shortcomings of my assignment and that my only hope was an early reassignment. To my total surprise, I received the only promotion I ever had in the foreign service—from foreign service officer class II to class I, an action that the FSO inspectors recommended!

Looking back on the two years I spent in IO, I must admit I was probably unfair to Francis Wilcox, my immediate supervisor and to my staff. They were all dedicated civil servants—dedicated to the principle of using multilateral solutions to solve the problems of the world. I am afraid I could never kindle much of a flame of enthusiasm for this approach. Nonetheless, I certainly appreciated the kind words of the political deputy assistant secretary, who congratulated me on the promotion with the words, "You deserve it."

It was my old teacher at the VOA, Foy Kohler, now assistant secretary of state for European Affairs, who rescued me from the doldrums of my office in Virginia. He asked me to become executive director of the European Bureau. Although once again it was not a job that political or economic officers in the foreign service would seek, it was a job that carried a lot of clout, particularly if the assistant secretary backed his executive director. The clout came from the fact that the executive director controlled, to a degree, the budget for the Bureau as well as the embassies in his area. In my case that included all of our embassies and consulates in Europe and Canada. He also had the capability, if he so chose to exercise it, of directing and assigning foreign service personnel.

I came to personally know more FSOs in this assignment than any time thereafter. Moreover, what Ambassador Thompson had predicted upon his leaving Vienna—"You'll get known in Washington"—now came about. Working on the one hand with the assistant secretary for administration, the director general of the foreign service, and the Foreign Service Inspection Corps, and on the other, with the assistant secretary of the European Bureau and the chiefs of mission (our ambassadors in Europe and Canada) made my name well known.

I made two major inspection trips during my stint as executive director, which gave me a good insight into how our embassies functioned. I learned who the good ambassadors were and who did not maintain good control over the diverse elements in nearly every embassy. I noted that morale among FS personnel was frequently higher at so-called hardship posts than at the plush fleshpots of London, Paris, and Rome. I could see first-hand the problems arising from our practice of appointing men and women to ambassadorships who had had no previous experience in diplomacy, but had contributed heavily to the coffers of the political party in power in the United States. On the other hand, career ambassadors, with little or no previous training in administration, found it difficult to ride herd on the many representatives of other agencies than the State Department, who were found particularly at our larger embassies. There were twenty-eight Washington agencies represented in our London embassy during my stint as executive director. Their combined personnel was much greater than that of the State Department.

As executive director I was present and participated in the meetings of the bureau chaired by the assistant secretary. Since I had never been accused of diffidence, I did not hesitate to comment on some of the remarks of my colleagues heading the geographic desks, an action, which, I am sure, did not always endear me to them.

It was heady stuff and I thoroughly enjoyed the job. It was a complete turnaround from my days in IO.

But five years in Washington was enough. Moreover, my benefactor, Foy Kohler, had moved on, and I wanted out. There was a job that opened up, which appealed to me very much. This was the number two position—deputy chief of mission—in Belgrade, Yugoslavia. The new president, John F. Kennedy, had recalled one of the finest diplomats in the annals of American diplomacy, George Kennan, from his duties at Princeton University to be ambassador to Yugoslavia. Kennan was regarded as one of the real experts in the field of United States-Soviet relations. He had been ambassador to Moscow in the middle of the Cold War. Upon leaving his post, for consultations in Washington, he was asked by correspondents in Berlin for an opinion of the USSR. His frank reply—that the atmosphere in Moscow reminded him of the situation in Nazi Germany in 1942—led to his being declared *persona non grata* in Moscow.

Kennan left diplomacy to become a professor at Princeton. Now President Kennedy called him back. He responded affirmatively and became United States ambassador to Yugoslavia. I was sent out to be looked over as his DCM, his executive officer, and I took my wife along. We spent some three days with the distinguished ambassador and his wife. It was readily apparent to me that he needed no political advice from me but that he could use my administrative abilities. We talked at great length, and at the end of our stay, he agreed to accept me as his deputy. My wife even looked at the deputy's house and took measurements for curtains. I was very happy I was going as number two to the most highly regarded Sovietologist at the time.

I was surprised no end—*shocked* would be a better word—when I was accosted in the halls of the State Department by a member of personnel who asked me if I would be interested in going to Bangkok, Thailand, as DCM. All I knew about Thailand was what I had seen from watching Yul Brynner in *The King and I* and said as much.

It was explained to me that the new United States

ambassador to Thailand, Kenneth Young, a protegé of Chester Bowles, and cast a bit in the mold of John Kennedy, was running amok in Bangkok and the foreign service was casting about for a strong officer with experience in administration to ride herd on the ambassador. This was not at all a pleasant prospect for a number-two man. My mind was set on Belgrade, but personnel pressed me to accept the number two job in Bangkok, but not until I had been found acceptable to Ambassador Young. He was in the State Department on consultation and a meeting was arranged for him to look me over.

His first question to me was, why did I want to go to Bangkok? My answer, quite frankly, was I didn't, but I had been asked to go by personnel. He inquired what I knew about Southeast Asia. I replied that I knew virtually nothing about that part of the world. In retrospect, this may have been the factor that made him accept me: He didn't want someone who was better versed than he in Southeast Asian affairs.

To make a long, quite pleasant interview short, he accepted me and notified personnel accordingly. I had mixed feelings. I was giving up the opportunity to work with one of the keenest minds in the annals of American diplomacy for a job in a part of the world I didn't know anything about with an American ambassador who really didn't have the confidence of the State Department. On the other hand, here was an opportunity to experience a part of the world totally unknown to me. I naturally bowed to the dictates of personnel.

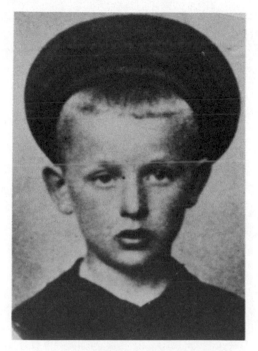

The author as a boy in his native Germany.

Changing of the guard. U.S. and Soviets shake hands, 1954.

The signers of the Austrian State Treaty on the balcony of Belvedere Palace. *Left to right:* French Foreign Minister Pinay, Soviet Foreign Minister Molotov, Austrian Foreign Minister Figl, U.S. Secretary of State John Foster Dulles, U.K. Foreign Secretary Harold MacMillan.

Vice President Nixon greets Viennese during December 1956 visit to Vienna. Author with scarf, left of Nixon.

Nixon meets Austrian foreign minister Dr. Leopold Figl. Author leaning over Nixon's shoulder. U.S. Ambassador Llewellyn F. Thompson, *right*. 1956.

The author and his wife with Ambassador Kenneth Young, Bangkok, 1962.

The author and his wife greeted by Thai Prime Minister Sarit, 1963.

The author with Chief Abbot of That Phanom, Thailand, 1963.

The author with His Royal Highness Prince Wan at Fourth of July reception, Bangkok, 1963.

The author with secretary general of SEATO, Bangkok, 1964.

The author with Prime Minister Thanom Kittikachorn, Bangkok, 1964.

Private citizen Nixon greeted by the author upon his arrival in Bangkok, 1964.

Nixon greeting Thai royalty, 1964.

The author and family en route home from Thailand, 1964.

President Johnson greets author, Washington, D.C.

**Secretary of State Dean Rusk greets German parliamentarians, 1968.**

## THE VICE PRESIDENT

WASHINGTON

December 13, 1968

Dear Al:

One of the privileges of being Vice President
has been the opportunity to work with you and
your colleagues. In the foreign affairs field,
few people have been more helpful to me than
yourself. Whether it was in relation to the
deliberations of the National Security Council
or to some of my overseas trips, you always
responded readily. I will long remember your
excellent work. In the months ahead I look
forward to continuing our association and friendship.

My best wishes to you and your family for a Merry
Christmas and a Happy New Year.

Sincerely,

Hubert H. Humphrey

Mr. Alfred Puhan
Deputy Assistant Secretary for
  European Affairs
Department of State
Washington, D. C.  20520

The author with President Losonczi at New Year's reception, Budapest, 1970.

The author and his wife with pianist Andre Watts, Budapest, 1970.

*Facing page:* A thank-you letter from Vice President Humphrey.

The author welcomes Hungarian Prime Minister Jeno Fock to the U.S. pavillion, Budapest Fair, 1972.

The author with Deputy Foreign Minister and Bank of Hungary Vice President Fekete at opening of U.S. exhibition, Budapest, 1973.

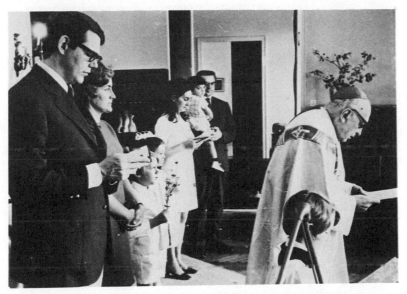

Cardinal Mindszenty saying Mass in the U.S. embassy, Budapest.

The Ambassador and the Cardinal, Budapest.

Secretary of State William P. Rogers with the author and Hungarian
Foreign Minister Janos Peter, *right,* arriving in Budapest, 1972.

Jeanne Lamar, the future Mrs. Puhan.

The author wishing a good trip to U.S. Deputy Foreign Minister Nagy. Deputy prime minister (back to camera) leading Hungarian party. Budapest, 1973.

*Left to right*: Senator Beall (Maryland), Senator Cannon (Nevada), the author, Deputy Foreign Minister Nagy, Budapest, 1973.

# Bangkok

In a brand new, white Studebaker, with air conditioning—the first we had ever had—we set out on a trip from Washington to San Francisco for my assignment to Bangkok. My oldest daughter cried most of the way across the country. She had reached the age where friendships with other girls were very important, and now she had to break all of those. While children in the foreign service probably gain more from living abroad with people of other nationalities and races, they also suffer some heart-wrenching experiences by being moved around every so often. This is especially true when they reach their teens.

In San Francisco we boarded one of the big planes for Tokyo, and there transferred to another headed for Bangkok. The ambassador and his wife were at the airport to greet us and take us to our hotel, the Erawan.

The ambassador was a kind, generous man. But he was not the easiest man to work with. Some of his ideas, like holding press conferences, with his small children clambering over him, startled journalists. And his ideas of doing things, which I thought were none of our business, bothered me. Moreover, I was being pressured by Washington to try to rein him in, which was something almost impossible for a number two to do.

135

I learned quickly that the problems of Thailand were not difficult to understand. Thailand was a country with a long history of neutrality, until her invasion by the Japanese in World War II. Thailand was a Third World country with rich natural resources but plagued by disease and corruption. Thailand was no great problem for the U.S. Of course, there had been Dien Bien Phu and the French defeat in neighboring Vietnam. Now, thanks to John Foster Dulles and the Eisenhower Administration, we had picked up the gauntlet where the French had dropped it. And Vietnam was just ahead.

I enjoyed Bangkok. It was a totally new experience for me. It was so different from anything I had ever experienced in Europe. I liked the Thai people. I got to know the dictator Sarit and his very intelligent foreign minister, Thanat Khoman, and found them very easy to talk to. I found a number of Thai nobles at the royal court, who had had their training in Berlin, and who spoke excellent German. Moreover, my experience in Austria gave me easy access to Austrian and German journalists now working in Vietnam.

We had a lovely home and had a huge screened-in porch where we could watch the little lizards (little newts called chin chucks) play and listen to the geckos.

Our health in Bangkok was generally good, though once every month I could count on a severe case of diarrhea, brought on usually by attending diplomatic functions, where the usual precautions—washing of hands, et cetera—were not observed. I never had a problem visiting villages where our arrival was expected. Long tables, laden with goodies, were set up in the main street. Naturally, one avoided any uncooked foods—raw pork, raw fish—and ate boiled rice with boiled chicken and hot tea.

Life in the Far East was not without its surprises. I recall one trip to a provincial town in Thailand, where we were housed in a government guest house. Upon getting up and going down for breakfast, we were faced with a bountiful breakfast of bacon and eggs—all stone-cold!

I found the Thai people most interesting. Starting at the top, Sarit, the dictator, was a fascinating man, and was reportedly the master of a harem of sixty to seventy girls. His successor, Thanom Kittikachorn, was a genial, pleasant man with whom I established a most cordial relationship. The foreign minister, Thanat Khoman, of Chinese origin, was a very astute, able official with whom I enjoyed many conversations. As for the nonofficial Thai, it was more difficult to establish relationships with them, but I managed to do so with the owner of an antique store and with several businessmen on the golf course.

The Thai are inveterate gamblers. On the Royal Bangkok Sports Club golf course, they would bet on virtually anything—who got closest to hole, who was first on the green, who had the lowest score, et cetera. Their conversations dwelled chiefly on three themes—women, money, and women! Politics was taboo!

I took Thai lessons and learned some of the rudiments of this difficult Chinese tongue. Occasionally this got me into trouble. One such time was when General Curtis LeMay, the tough chief of the United States Air Force paid an official visit to Thailand. He was entertained by the Thai air marshal at their club near the airport. I found myself seated between two ladies—wives of Thai air force officers. This was a rare occurrence, by the way, since Thai wives seldom appeared at social functions, and to make matters worse, they spoke not one word of English. I used every one of my five hundred words of Thai, and since the Thai language is a tonal language, where one word, pronounced differently, can mean two very different things. I obviously said some things that titillated these ladies. They burst into laughter and shrugged their pretty shoulders—no, no, no!

The stabilizing factor in Thailand is the King and Queen. Dictators may come and go, governments may change, but the king and queen of Thailand remain their rocks of stability.

It is not often the case that number-two officers in an embassy can get to know the king and queen of a country. But in my case, there was a reason. My ambassador, his wife and my wife, in a space of less than a week, all came down with hepatitis. It happened after we returned from a trip to the south of the country. Luckily I was spared. Indeed, officers in the embassy kept checking my pulse, since I was the only one of the four who did not contract the disease. The disease terminated Ambassador Young's tour in Thailand and left my wife debilitated—indeed, she never fully recovered her earlier strength as a result of her hepatitis.

For the next six months, his hepatitis complicated by a gastrointestinal affliction, Mr. Young never resumed his post. He was eventually moved to Manila and then sent home—he never returned. I was left in charge of the embassy for the next six months.

During this interim I had the opportunity to visit neighboring Cambodia upon the invitation of U.S. Ambassador Philip Sprouse. This fine man, a North Carolinian, and I believe, a confirmed bachelor, a great cook, and an old China hand, invited us down to Phnom Penh. We went for a marvelous visit. Phil Sprouse told me something I never forgot. To be a good cook, you have to first be able to scramble eggs properly and be able to make a good soup. He also gave me good advice. "You have been chargé for some time now. Remember when a new ambassador comes you have to adjust to him—not he to you." Thanks to Phil Sprouse we saw Angkor Wat before it was taken over by the communists. The trip to Angkor Wat and our stay there was a highlight of our assignment to Bangkok. We explored at leisure these ancient remnants of a great civilization.

While I was enjoying this novel exposure to a new world and new civilization, our children enjoyed Bangkok. They were able to commandeer the rickshas (*samlors*) of Bangkok, eat the stuff sold by the street vendors, ride at the Royal Bangkok Sports Club, and enjoy the international school there.

I played golf at the Royal Bangkok Sports Club, often with ambassadors of other countries. We had great matches. Torrential rains soaked us, but never stopped us from playing. A drink of Singha, a Thai beer introduced by German brewers, on the patio of the beautiful Royal Bangkok Sports Club was a real treat after a round of so-so golf.

These were idyllic days. I enjoyed the new and very different environment. To be sure, I was bothered occasionally by the pressure from Washington. This time it came from Averill Harriman, who wanted to rein in this ambassador, but the latter and I got along quite well. Indeed, some years after he had left the service, and I was stationed in Washington, we met at the wedding of the daughter of a mutual friend. I said to Ambassador Young that I sincerely appreciated the liberal education he had offered me in allowing me to travel all over Southeast Asia. With a smile he said it wasn't all altruistic. He hadn't really wanted me to look over his shoulder while he was in Bangkok. Kenneth Young was a good man. He was highly motivated and was interested in doing a good job as he perceived it. I found it difficult at times to agree with his actions, but I served him loyally.

This even extended to taking his place in a submarine participating in a war exercise with the Thai Navy in the Gulf of Siam. I flew down to the gulf with a young major in a small seaplane. The landing was smooth enough and the boarding of the sub was easily accomplished. Then we submerged. What I remember of the three or four hours we stayed under was the all-pervasive smell of diesel fuel and the odor of sweating men. The men ate well—most of them were overweight. There was the constant ping-ping of "hits" or "near-hits" on the sub from the ships above. I was relieved to have the experience behind me when we surfaced and I could smell fresh air as the hatch was opened! There still remained the harrowing experience of taking off in a sea now much rougher than when we landed in the morning. When we were finally airborne, I asked the perspiring pilot whether he had any doubts that we might not make it. He said nonchalantly, "Affirmative."

Undoubtedly the biggest dividend I reaped from my stay in Thailand was the opportunity to see most of Southeast Asia. As I mentioned earlier, the ambassador told me at the beginning of our association that he saw little point in both of us being at the embassy when he was in residence. He suggested that I take the old C-47 (DC-3) and the two deputy air force attaches on the staff of the embassy and see, not only Thailand but also the neighboring countries. Then when he traveled, I should mind the store. It was a superb arrangement.

I did not have to be reminded twice to carry out his suggestion. We visited all the major—and some not-so-major—towns of Thailand, frequently landing on a grassy strip after chasing water buffalo off the runway. With a young language officer as my companion, we called on local authorities—governors, mayors, abbots, monks, et cetera. We slept under mosquito netting in temples. We ate from long tables set up in dusty streets (avoiding the raw pork and fish) and sticking to rice, cooked meat, and beer.

I recall most vividly a visit we paid on a hill tribe in Northwest Thailand, above Chiangmai, in the hills on the Burma-Thai border. Our guide and mentor was a young missionary, whose father and grandfather had been missionaries in the Golden Triangle. We climbed in a jeep from the humid tropics into a much cooler atmosphere. There before us lay a plateau, with literally hundreds of tribesmen kicking up the dust with their dancing. Our guide took us to the chief of the tribe. I noticed that he, like all the other tribesmen, was chewing betel nuts with spittle dripping red from the corners of his mouth. Now I knew, of course, that in this part of the world the common greeting was the "wai," the putting together of the hands as if in prayer. (The higher the rank of the person being greeted, the higher the hands are raised.) So I was prepared to greet the chief with the customary "wai" but some European or American had apparently told the chief that one greeted a Westerner by shaking hands. Thus the chief first spat a mouthful of betel juice into his hands, and then, after casting the juice aside, extended his hand to me. I didn't blanch as I felt the betel nut juice squirt in my hand. I could hardly wait to get to the first available stream to wash my hands!

Our trips were not limited to the Thai towns and villages. I saw the pagodas of Rangoon and Mandalay in Northern Burma; visited Vientiane, the capital of Laos; and explored much of Vietnam in the company of Frank Pace, then secretary of the army. On the latter trip, as well as on one to Burma, we flew commercial planes and my wife accompanied me. We spent a couple of days at the Inn in the Cameron Highlands, from which some years later, Jim Thompson, the redeveloper of the Thai silk industry, disappeared on a walk. No one, to my knowledge, has ever seen or heard from him since.

The air attaché's plane had to be serviced occasionally and this was done at the great American military base in the Philippines. We spent a vacation at Camp John Hay and had a chance to get in some golf.

If this sounds as though I was seldom in the embassy, the fact was that Ambassador Young did a great deal of traveling himself, and I was quite often in charge of the embassy, which proved to be good training for what was to follow. The embassy was a very large one, with a huge Military Assistance Group (MAAG) and a very large Agency for International Development (AID) group. I chaired many meetings with generals or AID administrators. The experience I had gained at the Voice of America in administering large groups of personnel came in handy.

There was a hiatus of nearly six months, when the embassy had no ambassador, and I acted as chargé d'affaires. In the summer of 1963 we learned that a new ambassador to Thailand had been named.

This able career officer had begun his career in the administrative side of the foreign service in Paris, I believe. He had risen to the post of ambassador in Geneva to the European U.N. community. Indeed, when I was executive director of EUR, I had stopped off at his residence and met him and his wife. I had no reason to feel apprehensive about our future association. There were, however, a number of letters to me from friends, commiserating with my lot, but ending on the upbeat note:

if anybody can get along with the new ambassador, it was Al Puhan. I set to work to write a detailed account of the work of the embassy, its personnel, relations with the Thai, problems we had in Thailand, et cetera, and sent it to him.

When the ambassador and his wife arrived—some considerable time after his confirmation by the United States Senate—in the fall of 1963 I rented a river boat from one of my Thai Navy friends and invited the entire staff of the embassy aboard to meet the new chief of mission. A very intense man who smoked constantly, he was generally dour and distant. We began our association of nearly one year with my presentation of the ambassador to the top officers of the embassy at the weekly staff meeting. It was to be the only staff meeting ho attended during my stay in Bangkok. I invariably went to his office before each meeting to invite him, but he always said, "You take it." I made notes of the meeting each time and promptly sent them to him. They came back with a small check mark, indicating his having read them.

The country team concept—a regular meeting of the ambassador, his deputy, the principal officers of the embassy, the general commanding MAAG, the chief and deputy of the AID group, the head of the information program, and the CIA station chief—had been established to assure the cooperation of all elements in a large embassy like the one in Bangkok. A secondary purpose was to keep all segments of the mission informed of what was being done. Ken Young had met regularly with the country team and I had carried on the practice during the hiatus. When I informed the new ambassador of the date of the next country team meeting, he said that there would be no country team meetings during his tenure. He explained that the country team concept tended to dilute the ambassador's prerogative and he would have none of that. I was a bit taken aback by this decision, but said, "Well, you're the boss." And there were no more country team meetings as long as I was in Bangkok. The ambassador obviously preferred to deal with each head of department on a one-on-one basis.

In the early days of our association I spent much time in his office, briefing him and accompanying him on the calls he made on the top Thai authorities. I began to wonder why he spent so much time dwelling on the duties of the ambassador—pulling books from the bookcase and citing the ambassador's responsibilities and relations with Washington. As the days grew into weeks, I realized that he and I were not meant for each other. There appeared to be an inability to communicate—at least on my part. I searched my own mind and lay awake at night, trying to fathom what I was doing wrong. I recalled Ambassador Sprouse's warning: "Remember, it's the duty of the deputy to adjust to the chief of mission, and not the other way around." I had been frank and open with the ambassador since his arrival and had undertaken no action affecting the embassy without prior notification to him and getting his approval.

I decided that my outgoing nature and easy relationships with the Thai and other diplomatic missions in the city, combined with the reticent and almost reclusive nature of the ambassador's behavior, may have accounted for the relationship that grew more difficult with each passing day.

Life was not easy for me. I had many inquiries from the Thai and others why they saw nothing or very little of the ambassador, inquiries that I sought to deflect by saying the ambassador was busy reading up on the problems of US-Thai relations and would surely play a more prominent role in the near future.

One incident troubled me in particular. The occasion was the annual Armed Forces Day, hitherto attended by the chief of mission, his military attaches, the Thai dictator, the foreign minister and other high-ranking Thai military and civilian personnel. I told the ambassador that he would probably be called upon to make a few remarks. To my astonishment he said, "You go."

I, of course, went and not unexpectedly found the following day's newspapers replete with pictures of the Thai dictator and me on the front pages.

I realized that my days with the ambassador were limited on the night that we received the news of President Kennedy's assassination. The duty officer in the embassy had called the ambassador who hurried there. I was not informed by the ambassador or the duty officer of President Kennedy's death until the following morning.

The ambassador began to use the air force attaché, a very action-oriented man, as a kind of ambassadorial aide. He did the same thing with a political-military officer, a career foreign service officer, who very loyally came to my office each time to inform me what the ambassador had said and wanted done.

Near the end of 1963, I pleaded fatigue from a long stint as chargé and asked the ambassador if my wife and I could take a brief vacation. He posed no objection, and we went to Japan. I had to sort out my thoughts about the past few months and the future. I rationalized that if the ambassador had wanted a man of his choice in the deputy's spot, he could have asked the State Department for such a person. That was certainly his prerogative and he had not exercised it. I made up my mind to continue to work loyally for him, but that when my original tour of duty of two years ended, I would ask him for a transfer.

The next six months—until midsummer 1964—were the most difficult in my life. I tried in every possible way to assist the ambassador and do the job of executive officer as he had a right to expect. All my efforts were met with either a noncommittal remark or no comment at all. Fortunately, the staff of the embassy, with one single exception, remained loyal to me, even though they could see that the ambassador was treating me like a fifth wheel on a wagon.

I had experienced other low points in my career—the early days in Vienna, the assignment to Washington as deputy director of OIA—but nothing compared to the last six months of my stay in Thailand. Indeed, my health began to suffer.

Shortly before the end of my tour of duty I went in to inform the ambassador that I felt it would be better for all if I asked for a transfer and give him the opportunity to select his own deputy. His laconic reply was "Suit yourself." Just before we left in July of 1964, the ambassador said he wanted to give a farewell party for us and suggested I get up a list of guests—all the people I had dealt with. I came up with a list of six hundred suggested guests. They all came.

I probably would have regarded this relationship between ambassador and deputy a closed chapter, once away from Bangkok, if it hadn't been for an action by my former chief, which I felt was most unkind. It concerned the efficiency or fitness report that had to be prepared annually by every supervisor in the embassy. The promotion panel in Washington, headed by a distinguished ambassador, discovered that there was no report made on my work during the two years I had served in Bangkok. He asked me how this had happened. I could account for the absence of a report from Ambassador Young, since he was ill at the time the report was due, and now had left government service. I could not, however, account for the absence of a report from the current ambassador.

The head of the promotion panel sent a cable to the ambassador, inquiring about a report on me. Back came the puzzling reply that a reading of the *New York Times* would explain the absence of a report. Asked for a possible explanation of the ambassador's reply, I suggested that the ambassador's preoccupation with the fast-growing build-up of American forces in Thailand and Vietnam—reported daily in the *New York Times*—left him no time for such a report, and I suggested that I would not press him.

The ambassador heading the panel thought otherwise and instructed the ambassador in Bangkok to prepare a report on me. There came a lengthy cable, not the regular efficiency report, in which the ambassador spoke of the difficult relationship between him and me, and gallantly accepted the blame for this poor state of affairs. His analysis of my work contained such statements as "this officer would probably perform better as a chief of a small mission than 50 percent of the officers in his class." He went on to add that I had a predilection for military matters (not so), but didn't get along well with the military (not so) since I even got along very well with Generals Harkins and Westmoreland, who shared my office when they came to Bangkok, or with Admiral Felt, Commander-in-Chief Pacific Fleet. In this rather devious manner the ambassador doomed my career, had it not been for the fact that I was well known by now in Washington, and so was he.

I met the ambassador several times after my departure from Bangkok. On all of these occasions he went out of his way to be courteous and indeed kind. When he learned some years later while he was ambassador in Rome that my wife and I were planning a vacation in Sicily, he insisted that we be his guests in Rome. It was a unique evening. While his wife and mine spent the evening talking to Billy Graham, a houseguest of the ambassador, he spent his time talking to me. I was an ambassador myself at that point. It almost seemed to me that he was trying to make amends for his behavior toward me in Bangkok.

Bangkok in retrospect was a great new experience for me. Thailand is a wonderfully beautiful country. Its smiling people are easy to cultivate. The peacefulness of Thailand is, however, occasionally shattered by brutality and cruelty. It was not unusual for a bus driver involved in an accident to run from the scene and go into hiding rather than accept any responsibility.

Thailand had preserved her neutrality and sovereignty for centuries. The old capitals of Chiangmai and Ayuthia, with their *wats* (temples) spoke of a golden age centuries ago. Bangkok and Thonburi, on the opposite side of the Chao Prya River, were the most recent capitals of Thailand.

Thailand's principal problem after the invasion of the country by the Japanese was her hinterlands. Most Thai doctors, teachers and public servants, many of whom were trained in the United States, were wedded to the capital city. Few wanted to have anything to do with the country outside of Bangkok. A large group of Vietnamese living in the northeast of the country were a potential danger to Bangkok.

The peasants living in the country were easy prey for communist agitators. The only contact the peasants had with the capital was by way of the tax collector, who was naturally a hated individual.

While I was in Thailand, the country was just beginning to be the site for the American build-up in the Vietnam war. But much of that was to take place after I had left Bangkok.

# *Germany*

**W**HEN we left Thailand, I found myself in the same position so many other FSOs found themselves—and still do today: I had no assignment. There seemed to me no need to hurry, because quite likely I was destined to walk the halls of the State Department and shop for a job. Consequently, we booked passage on the SS *President Wilson* from Yokohama to San Francisco, with a layover in Hawaii.

In Honolulu, one of the three deputy assistant secretaries of European Affairs reached me by telephone in our hotel room. He informed me that I had been named director of the Office of German Affairs and that I should appear in the State Department as quickly as possible.

While a Washington assignment did not strike me as the most desirable posting at the time, the fact that our children were growing up and would profit from attendance in our public schools helped to reconcile me to a Washington assignment. And the more I thought about it, my assignment to direct German affairs seemed so natural, what with my knowledge of the language and my German background. I learned some time later that when personnel used the computer to come up with the best qualified candidates for the assignment, two names were at the top: William R. Tyler, then assistant secretary of state for European Affairs, and mine, Alfred Puhan.

In spite of the order to appear posthaste in Washington, I knew that August was not a month in which much business was done both in Europe and in Washington. I made one concession, and that was to fly from Honolulu to San Francisco rather than continue by sea. However, we had ordered a car for delivery in San Francisco and traveled by auto across the country, giving the children and us an opportunity to see for the second time much of the United States.

I recalled that we arrived in Washington on a Saturday, and on Monday, bright and early, I reported to my new chief, William R. Tyler, the assistant secretary of state for European Affairs. He was somewhat astonished to see me so early, reminding me that August was not a month of great activity! We settled in Virginia, first in a rental and then a charming house in McLean. The children were enrolled in the public schools of that lovely bit of suburban Washington, D.C., and I began my commuting from there to the State Department in Foggy Bottom at least six times each week and sometimes seven.

The Office of German Affairs, when I was placed in charge, did not control all German affairs. When the Russians and East Germans erected the Berlin Wall in 1961, a special task force had been established—headed by the assistant secretary himself—to deal with the crisis posed by the erection of the infamous wall.

Now, in 1964, the task force, as constituted, had little to do, and when bureaucrats find themselves without work, they make work. More and more the Berlin Task Force had become the tail that wagged the dog. Fairly aggressive leadership by the director of the task force combined with weak leadership of the Office of German

Affairs left many of the more important aspects of United States-German relations in the hands of the former.

It didn't take me long to see that this situation would have to change if a well-coordinated policy toward Germany was to be pursued. The assistant secretary for European Affairs agreed with my reasoning, and the Berlin Task Force was integrated into the Office of German affairs. It was greatly reduced in size and met only whenever there was a Berlin crisis, and then was chaired by the director of the Office of German Affairs.

U.S.-German relations were an important element in American foreign policy during the Johnson administration. Not only was the Federal Republic of Germany, with its capital in Bonn, rapidly emerging as the most important nation in NATO, the defensive alliance forged years earlier to protect the West from potential aggression by the Soviet Union, but it also was the base for thousands of American forces. We supported the fiction of *Wiedervereinigung*—the joining of West and East Germany at "some time in the future," while at the same time not really welcoming such a reunion. There probably was not a single country in either the western or eastern camp that desired the reunion of the two Germanys. Many Germans themselves feared the revival of a strong, united Germany. However, relations with the Soviet Zone—or East Germany, or the Soviet Zone of Occupation, as the future German Democratic Republic was called—were governed by what was known as the Hallstein Doctrine. Simply put, this meant that the Bonn government would suspend relations with any state that recognized the East German regime. Since the Federal Republic had nearly three times the population of the Soviet Zone, and already was a powerful economic state, the future German Democratic Republic (GDR) was recognized only by the Soviet puppets and some Third World countries.

The flashpoint of our relations with Germany was Berlin. The former capital of the Reich, still largely in ruins, particularly the Soviet Sector, had, like Vienna, been placed under four-power occupation with an Allied Commission to govern the city. As part of the consolidation of its empire in the second half of the forties by throwing out the coalition governments in Eastern Europe and putting its own puppets in the governments of those countries, the Soviet Union sought to include East Germany in the process. They terminated the Allied Commission, or their participation in it, and tried to eject the Americans, British, and the French from Berlin. The result was the Berlin blockade, which failed because of the steadfastness of the western allies and the supplying of the city by means of the historic Berlin airlift. This was the most strenuous effort by the Soviets to make all of Berlin the capital of the GDR. There were periodically efforts to eject the western allies from Berlin by blockading the land route from the Federal Republic to Berlin or harassing U.S. and British planes flying the narrow corridors alloted to the allies by the document establishing the Allied Commission at the end of WW II. This invariably led to the so-called Berlin crises. All of these Soviet-East German efforts were foiled, but not without some cost to us.

The once-great city of Berlin began to show signs of decay. Young Berliners saw no future in staying in the capital and emigrated to the thriving cities of the Federal Republic. There were fears that Berlin would become an old-age sanatorium.

This situation was complicated by the West German position on Berlin. Although no Lufthansa planes could fly to Berlin, the Federal Republic maintained that the city was a "land," a province of the FRG. This posture was, of course, totally rejected by the Soviets, but was not accepted by us either. The FRG would occasionally dispatch its president to Berlin or attempt to hold West German government meetings in the city, actions which we did not prevent from taking place, but which invariably led to Soviet threats.

When I took over as director of the Office of German Affairs in 1964, the West German economic miracle, the *"Wirtschaftswunder"* was well under way. The infusion of U.S. aid—the Marshall Plan combined with German industry—saw German cities rebuilt, and historic buildings lovingly restored with their original bricks pulled from the ruins. Factories with the newest machines were built, and Germans began to live well again.

There was, however, a malaise in the country—a feeling that however strong Germany was economically it had no political role to play. Germans frequently complained that they were a huge body with a tiny, pinpoint head. This mood, shared by the German politicians, required frequent assurance that the FRG was indeed important. Scarcely a week passed during my five years as director of German Affairs that I did not receive a delegation of German parliamentarians, businessmen, or journalists. A friend once asked me what I told them. I replied that I greeted them, welcomed them to Washington, and then spent the next hour or two listening. All of them wanted to see the president, of course, but since he and his secretary of state, Dean Rusk, were increasingly preoccupied with Vietnam, I could usually depend upon the genial vice-president, Hubert H. Humphrey, to see them for a few minutes. It was second-best, but it usually did the trick.

Every West German Chancellor since Adenauer, whom I visited during the last year of his long life in Bonn, felt the necessity to make a pilgrimage to America. Ludwig Erhard, frequently called the father of the West German *"Wirtschaftswunder"* became the favorite German chancellor of Lyndon Johnson. Together with the president he went to the latter's Texas ranch, donned a cowboy hat, and heartily ate Texas-style barbecue.

Indeed, after Erhard had left office, he came on a visit to the U.S. President Johnson wanted to tender a luncheon for him and I was asked to get up a guest list of some thirty or forty prominent Americans, who might at one time or another have had some connection with Germany. After preparing such a guest list, which included men like John J. McCloy and Lucius Clay, I put my name at the bottom of the list. When Erhard and his ubiquitous cigar arrived in Washington, I took him first to see Secretary of State Dean Rusk. After an exchange of some pleasantries, I mentioned to the secretary that it was time to get to the White House. Erhard left with the German Ambassador; the secretary went to his car, and I had a small black car at my disposal for this occasion.

There followed one of the more humorous incidents of my time in this job. I entered the White House grounds at the southwest corner and, with invitation in hand, was quickly passed through. As we drove up the long winding driveway to the south portico, I saw the tall Texan president standing under the canopy, ready to greet his favorite German, now an ex-chancellor. I told my driver not to stop at the door but to drive a few yards on. He either didn't hear me or didn't understand. In any event, there was the president of the United States opening the door for the director of the office of German Affairs! One glance at my midriff was sufficient to convince the president that I was not the rotund Erhard. Very pleasantly he greeted me with a friendly "How are you?" I thanked him and asked him how he was—fine. This was repeated two more times—once when Dean Rusk appeared, and again when Eugene Rostow, an undersecretary of state drove up.

The secretary beckoned me to follow him into the White House. As we passed a little anteroom, there sat the former chancellor and the German ambassador, chatting away merrily. They had entered the White House at the north entrance and nobody had told the president.

Kiesinger, who succeeded Erhard, made several trips to Washington. The secretary of state appeared at times to have little patience with the Germans, a trait he did not always conceal very well. I believe he felt very strongly that since we had helped the Germans back onto their feet, they should help us some with our undeclared war in Vietnam. He thought, and not unreasonably so, the least they could do was not be critical of our efforts.

Another of our problems with the Germans concerned the extent of supporting our troops on German bases. The pressure to get more support than we did came largely from the Senate. There were recurring threats, led by Senator Mike Mansfield, to greatly reduce the number of our troops, if not bring them all back home. These threats gave the Germans the jitters, for I am not sure they trusted themselves with their own ever-growing military establishment. Nor did they feel secure, living next door to the belligerent Soviets! The Dutch, Danes, Belgians, French, and other of our NATO allies also felt safer with a U.S. commitment of men and arms in Germany than with a German force of nearly half a million soldiers.

President Johnson attended Adenauer's funeral on April 24–26, 1967. I was a very junior member of the presidential party. Amidst the solemnity of the occasion were some amusing moments. One concerned the display of some mediocre German art on the lawn of our ambassador's residence arranged by the administrative elements in the Embassy and by the presidential party. The president made a review of the art and pointed to one or two he liked. They were bought for him.

I accompanied Vice-President Hubert Humphrey and his wife on a visit to Germany, which included a stopover in Berlin. As we were flying there Mr. Humphrey asked me if he was likely to be asked to make a speech in Berlin. I assured him that most certainly a battery of microphones would be set up in front of the city hall and that he would be expected to say something. It was a time when the president hoped to meet with the Russians and therefore no provocative remarks were in order. The vice-president asked what he should say. Having never seen Humphrey at a loss for words on any occasion, I assured him he would do all right.

He did. Faced by thousands of Berliners, he did not say "Ich bin ein Berliner" but he made a rousing speech that pleased Berlin. In fact, he spoke on six or seven more occasions that day in Berlin. When his work was done, the vice-president said, "Let's go dancing," and dance we did, well into the night.

The following day, flying out of Berlin, I was chatting with the vice-president when Muriel, his wife, called his attention to an editorial in the *Paris Herald Tribune* titled "LBJ needs HHH more than HHH needs LBJ." With a wry smile he said, "Well, that's probably the last trip we'll make for LBJ."

Hubert Humphrey was certainly one of the most gracious and loquacious politicians I ever met. After his trip to Berlin he wrote a "Dear Al" letter, stating, "If my trip had any measure of success, it was in large part due to your efforts." On another occasion, late in 1968, he wrote, "One of the privileges of being VP has been the opportunity to work with you. . . . In the foreign affairs field, few people have been more helpful to me than yourself."

A major problem we had was that there was so little that was positive we could talk about to our visitors. I recall the visit of German Chancellor Erhard in 1965. When our ambassador to Bonn called my office and complained that the only thing we could talk about was getting more money out of the Germans in support of our troops stationed in Germany, I remarked, half in jest, that the *Washington Post* had carried a headline to the effect that Congress had just cut funds for some of our space programs, including a solar probe. I thought maybe the Germans would like to take that on. He said, "Put that down on paper," which I did in a great hurry without proper staffing or clearance from my boss in the State Department. Imagine my surprise when the president that evening, in toasting the German Chancellor, suggested that the Germans take on the project of a solar probe. The next day, December 21, 1965, the *Washington Post* carried the front-page headline, "Johnson invites Erhard to join space ventures." I told my children that I had just made history.

Another spinoff of one of those visits was a study of both countries' waste disposal and pollution. The U.S. team that went to Germany was led by our secretary of the interior, Stuart Udall. Senator Muskie of Maine was a member of the delegation. We saw some fascinating projects, particularly in Munich, where Mayor Vogeler showed us that city's waste disposal system. I predicted at the time that Vogeler would one day become a leading German politician on the national scene, which indeed he has. We drank water from the Ruhr River, which had once been heavily polluted, but now was as pure and as clear as crystal.

We attended a large banquet, in Duesseldorf, I believe it was, where I noted on the heavily laden tables some steak tartar as well as a lighter ground raw meat. I asked my German tablemate what it was and was told it was raw pork. Somewhat astounded, I asked if the Germans were not afraid of getting trichinosis. His reply was that in the U.S. we had pigs that carried trichinosis but in Germany that was only rarely the case!

Wilbur Cohen, secretary of HEW, headed a delegation to Berlin to help open the new medical clinic that was financed in large part with U.S. funds to help the Berliners. I acted as his escort and interpreter—our names are in the Golden Book of the City of Berlin.

I accompanied secretary of state Dean Rusk on a trip to the annual NATO meeting, this time in Reykjavik, Iceland. The reason I was asked to accompany the secretary on this NATO trip was that there were to be important discussions with Willy Brandt, former mayor of Berlin, later vice chancellor, and finally, federal chancellor.

We worked hard—indeed we never noticed the ending of the day and the beginning of night in this far northern city. I recall driving home from our meetings at 4 or 5 A.M., still light enough on this June night to drive without lights.

Our meetings in Reykjavik concluded, we boarded the secretary's plane in the morning, flew to Cologne, sped by car to Bonn for meetings with the chancellor, vice chancellor, and the Mayor of Berlin. The secretary was not feeling well, and was fatigued when we met with the Berlin mayor. He was so weary in fact that I had to prompt him with answers.

Still on the same day, we sped back on the autobahn to Cologne, flew over the Atlantic, and arrived that same evening in Washington. I was relieved that it was a Friday and counted on catching up on my sleep the following day. The phone rang early on Saturday and the duty officer said that the secretary was calling a meeting at 9:00 A.M. to review our consultations with the Germans. Weary and bleary-eyed I roused myself out of bed and was in place when the secretary strode in, looking as fresh as ever.

In addition to the journeys I made with the top officials of our government to Germany, I made a number of trips by myself—visiting our consulates in Bremen, Hamburg, Frankfurt, Stuttgart, and Munich, as well as our mission in Berlin, and of course, the embassy itself. Having a complete command of the German language, I was able to sample public German opinion. I found early that the West Germans saw no hope of a reunited Germany, and were quite reconciled to the present state of affairs.

Much of my time in Washington was spent with ambassadors, both ours and the German ambassador in Washington. The latter, a genial man, not tainted by Nazism, did a great job for his country. Although reputedly not a favorite of President Kennedy, Ambassador Heinrich Knappstein did much to redeem Germany's reputation in the U.S. after Hitler and the holocaust. He traveled far and wide, visited synagogues, established good relations with Jewish organizations, and generally presented a picture of the good German. He was not a great diplomat in the old classical sense, but he was just

160

what Washington needed in a German ambassador at the time. I spent many hours with him and his principal aides, particularly Berndt von Staden, a brilliant diplomat, who later became German ambassador to Washington himself. This steady contact between the German embassy in Washington and myself was most useful in keeping relations between our two countries on an even keel.

Knappstein was not the only ambassador I had close dealings with in my job as director of the Office of German Affairs. The other was our U.S. Ambassador in Bonn, a freewheeling, dynamic Texas oilman. I served as the middleman between him and the secretary of state in Washington. The ambassador frequently tried out ideas of his on me to see whether they would float. He also always sent me the text of long speeches he made in Germany with the expectation that I would get them cleared in Washington, which was not always an easy task. In spite of the fact that I sometimes had to ask him to delete certain statements, we got along generally well. This in spite of the fact that occasionally Washington resorted to a practice that was to become commonplace—sending a special presidential envoy to Bonn without informing the ambassador.

Since there was no officer of higher rank and greater expertise on German affairs on the seventh floor of the State Department where the secretary of state had his office, I became in fact, Mr. Germany, the secretary's right-hand man on German affairs. I recall one day during my last year in Washington, when the assistant secretary had elevated me to the position of acting deputy assistant secretary of state with responsibility for Western European matters, the secretary asked me, in connection with some Franco-German problem, who was in charge of French affairs. I told him I was, and in astonishment he said, "No you are my German expert!"

To me the most interesting German chancellor was Willy Brandt whom I first met in Berlin when he was *"Oberbuergermeister"* (Lord Mayor). A German who had lived in Scandinavian exile during the war, where he also married, he became the chairman of the Socialist party, and with that party's victory, became chancellor. A man of many moods—some quite somber—he was by no means the favorite of the Washington establishment. His overtures to East Germany, somewhat ahead of those of the U.S., were feared as a move toward a neutral Germany. I never felt that that was his objective. He was realistic enough to see that the hostility between the two Germanys should cease in order that West Germans might visit their relations in East Germany. Brandt was the leading German exponent of detente, a policy to be espoused shortly by President Nixon and Henry Kissinger. When Brandt, as chancellor came to Washington (by-now a required journey of every German head of government), he was quite unhappy. I recall very vividly his appearance at a German embassy reception, with the secretary of state and other high-ranking U.S. government officials in attendance. He seemed to be going through the required paces, shaking a hand here and another there, with barely a smile on his face. He finally brightened considerably when he spotted me, someone whom he had known for some time. His lingering with me to talk—in German—began to cause me some embarrassment, since I felt he ought to be spending time with our higher-ranking guests.

Helmut Schmidt, successor to Brandt as chancellor, is a most interesting and complicated man. I met him, before he became head of government in Germany, in

Washington where he came to a meeting of the Atlantic Conference, a gathering of top German and U.S. officials with an interest in German and NATO affairs. Schmidt was known for speaking his mind—frequently caustically. I recall walking with him from one of Washington's leading hotels to a restaurant. The walk plus the talk at the luncheon were quite revealing. His comments were mostly about German and U.S. officials. I did not stay in my post long enough to see him become chancellor of the Federal Republic, but I could foresee problems which our government would have with this brilliant, outspoken man.

The recent Iran-Contra affair, which preoccupied our government and citizens in the summer of 1987, reminded me of the manner in which the National Security Council staff, the National security advisor and the White House staff operated in the sixties—twenty years earlier. These bodies, housed in the old State Department Building, the executive offices of the White House, operated in not so different a manner from the way they do now. The national security advisor and his staff, instead of having the cabinet secretaries do the ground work and then pull the various opinions together for the president's decision, became operational. Too many bright young officers found the pace of State Department recommendations too slow. I recall that I was asked on a number of occasions to come up with advice on German affairs. I was told, "Don't try to clear it through State channels, because we'll get it too late and too diluted by clearing officers." So while years have passed, presidents have come and gone, as have national security advisors, the problem remains. Add to that the fact that the president is invariably closest to the men and women who helped elect him, but who frequently lack the expertise in foreign affairs and distrust the State Department, and you have the makings of trouble. I suspect it was the California mafia that brought down the most intelligent and experienced president of the U.S. in the last half century.

Meanwhile, my children in McLean were growing up. In 1967 my oldest daughter, Ursula, married a classmate at Baldwin Wallace. My second daughter was in college at Radford. My son Fred went through the trials and tribulations of youth in the Vietnam years, but fortunately came out unscathed.

My mother died peacefully in her seventy-eighth year at the home of my younger sister. I felt fortunate that she had come to our house for the summer before her death in the fall. Widowed for sixteen years when she passed away and having a husband before his death who had become senile, she had lived a hard life. She raised four children and found time to take care of her oldest grandchild one summer, while my wife was pregnant with our son. For years she had taken care of my uncle and aunt in Sandwich, Illinois, both of whom were bedridden for years. Her reward was a contested will left by my aunt and uncle and a long trial that left most of the estate to the lawyers. My mother had enjoyed one trip to Europe—her first and only airplane trip. This was in 1956 while we were in Vienna. She looked up her only sister in West Germany who, with her husband and children, had survived WWII in Germany. However, she was not to live long enough to see me appointed ambassador of the United States, a wish she had devoutly expressed on a number of occasions. When she died, her estate came to roughly four thousand dollars, which she willed in equal installments to her four children. I thought that the most appropriate memorial I could leave for her was to put my thousand dollars as a downpayment on a green-house, since she had always loved flowers. The green-house was to serve me as a refuge some years later when my marriage fell apart.

During the last year of my five-year tour in Washington, the assistant secretary for European Affairs raised me to the level of acting deputy assistant secretary of state for Western European Affairs. In fact, except for a larger office, my duties changed little. German Affairs, now headed by my deputy, remained my principal concern. I left the management of the other West European countries in the hands of the people who headed the various desks. There were a few additional duties as a result of my elevation to a higher status.

One of them consisted of the supervision of State Department papers when a Dutch prime minister or an Italian head of government came on an official visit to Washington. Another was to accompany the vice-president, Spiro Agnew by this time, to the airport to receive heads of government and state upon the death of President Eisenhower. Still a third was the broadening of my social horizons. The embassies of the West European countries began to include me in their guest lists on national days and other occasions.

One of my strangest assignments as director of German Affairs had to do with the balance of payments problem (BALPA). The undersecretary of state asked me to visit a number of Far Eastern countries to see what reductions could be made by cutting personnel, an assignment which would not endear the officer thus charged. I traveled to Tokyo, Seoul, Taipei, Manila, and Bangkok. Everywhere there was stonewalling against any cuts in personnel, especially from the non-State Department personnel. A 10 percent cut in personnel was achieved, but unhappily, as was always the case, it came largely at the expense of the State Department and the foreign service.

I was now coming to the end of my fifth year in my job of shepherding German affairs. I was soon to be fifty-six years of age, and felt that if I was ever to achieve what every career officer seeks, namely an ambassador-ship, now was my last chance.

The 1968 election had brought Richard M. Nixon to the presidency. Since my work as escort officer for him in Austria, when he was vice-president twelve years earlier, I had seen him on a number of occasions. The first was after his defeat at the hands of the California voters when he ran for the governor's chair. I was the chargé d'affaires in Bangkok at the time. The Thais had a high regard for Nixon. After all, he had been Ike's vice-president, and that made him very much *persona grata*. However, he was a defeated candidate whose public life appeared to be behind him. Hence, only a protocol officer, my nine-year-old son and I were at the airport to greet him on this one of his many trips. Nixon was, of course, cordially received by the top Thai officials, but there was time for us to reminisce about our association in Vienna in 1956.

While in Washington, I had occasion to brief him once or twice prior to his trips to Europe while he was preparing himself for yet another try at the presidency. So it was no great surprise that I was elected to introduce the new German ambassador to the new president of the United States shortly after he had taken office. During that meeting, with only the new and totally inexperienced protocol chief present as the fourth person in the room, the president showed no sign of recognition for the first few minutes of the exchange of pleasantries. Only when the conversation turned to Berlin and I took out of my jacket pocket my ever-present notebook, did I see him glance in my direction. Suddenly he rose. The German ambassador thought the conversation was finished. He came over to me and said, "Where did we first meet—Berlin or Vienna?" When I said Vienna, the president turned to the ambassador and said, "You see, Mr. Ambassador, I have men like this all throughout our diplomatic service and I know I can count on their loyalty, so I am not worried about our conduct of foreign affairs."

The election of a Republican president brought new faces in all positions held by political appointees. This process was usually followed by what I always likened to two strange dogs meeting. They sniff each other suspiciously until they have both decided that neither intended to attack the other. The career officers who remain in place are the objects of suspicion of the incoming administration. They served the old administration, didn't they? Can they possibly be loyal to us?

My chief for the last two to three years was John Leddy, a most capable officer. A Democrat, he told me he would not work for Nixon. He asked me what my plans were. I told him that at fifty-five years of age, this was probably my last chance to become ambassador, a chief of mission. He was somewhat sceptical of my desire, saying that I could be much more useful in Washington than serving as a messenger boy somewhere outside of America. I told him that it was the goal of every career officer to cap his career with an ambassadorship.

When a president takes over, all career officers appointed by the president and confirmed by the Senate must resign. Not all resignations are accepted, although many are. One of the ambassadors who resigned was Martin Hillenbrand, a German expert who had received his ambassadorship some one-and-a-half years earlier.

He was the first U.S. ambassador to Hungary. His predecessors since WWII in Hungary had either been heads of legations (ministers) or chargé d'affaires. Hillenbrand had been selected to succeed Leddy as assistant secretary of state for European Affairs. This left an opening that appealed to me. Germany was out of the question because of my having been born there, and Vienna was sure to go to a political contributor to the election of the president. And Hungary, with its long association with Austria, a country in the Commonwealth of Soviet States, and the possibility of doing some good work seemed quite attractive. I mentioned this to outgoing Secretary Leddy, adding that the appointment of a German expert to the post Leddy was leaving made my continued presence in the department superfluous.

The naming of an ambassador requires the approval of what we irreverently called the "in-house" and the "out-house." The "in-house" was usually the most senior foreign service officer in place in the State Department. When I was named, this was a distinguished U.S. ambassador, U. Alexis Johnson. He had been, inter alia, ambassador to Thailand, had maintained an interest in that country, and knew of my work there. I got his approval quickly. The "out-house" in such cases is usually a high-ranking pol, someone well known to the president. Undoubtedly he will check with the White House any appointments made to the top jobs. In any event, whether Budapest was too insignificant or too unattractive to a political candidate, my nomination was approved early in 1969. The president readily signed it. My name and past associations with him had been refreshed by two meetings with him since he had entered the White House. The first I have already described when I presented the new German ambassador to him a few days after his taking office.

The second was a far more extensive meeting. Indeed, it lasted for some ten hours over a period of four days. The occasion was the briefing of the president prior to his first trip to Europe in March of 1969. Leddy was on his way out and I was designated to head the briefing team consisting of officers chairing the Belgian, German, Italian, French, and United Kingdom desks.

Faced by the president in the Cabinet Room, with the new secretary of state, William P. Rogers, at his right and a new national security advisor, Henry Kissinger, at his left, I briefed the president on Germany and added comments here and there when I thought they were required. It was a fascinating experience. President Nixon listened attentively for ten hours, a yellow pad in front of him, making notes now and then and asking rather penetrating questions. He was interrupted during those hours only twice—by telephone—which he answered quickly and then returned to the briefing.

It became clear to me early on that the president's central objective in taking this first of many trips he was to take was to change US-Franco relations. The Democratic administration of Lyndon Johnson had been so exercised by the haughty French president, Charles deGaulle, that the latter's name was never used around LBJ. Nixon, recognizing the importance of France to us, was about to change that. I could see his displeasure when the State Department officer in charge of the French Desk described our policy toward France.

During these long hours of briefing, the president showed himself, as he had in our earlier encounters with him, to be a good listener and an intelligent questioner who was well acquainted with the countries he was about

169

to visit. None of the charges made against him in later, unhappier years, such as the use of expletives and four-letter words was evident. Ever courteous and grateful for suggestions and advice from me and my team, the president struck me as probably the best-equipped man to enter upon this high office in this century to deal with the complex foreign relations of our country. I also deduced from these meetings that the president would, in all probability, seek to stabilize our relationship with the communist world.

Upon the conclusion of the briefings, the president held a press conference to which I was invited. Henry Kissinger, whom I had met while I was directing German affairs and he was still in academia, told me at the conference that the president had been greatly impressed with my presentation and that I was probably one of the best foreign service officers he had met. Kissinger added that he was pleased that I was going as ambassador to Hungary, but wished I were going to a post more important to us than Hungary. I said I thought I ought to serve my apprenticeship as chief of mission somewhere, and that if I performed well, I hoped to be considered for a more important post.

It is customary for a new ambassador to be sworn in before he leaves for his post. This ceremony, held in the beautiful lounge on the eighth floor of the State Department, is usually conducted by the chief of protocol. In my case, it was Secretary of State William P. Rogers himself who did me the honor, probably because he remembered me from his trip to Austria in 1956 with then Vice-President Nixon. Before some two hundred guests, he administered the oath of office, the same one taken by the president of the United States. After a few graceful words about me, the secretary turned the microphone over to me. Addressing the Hungarian ambassador to the U.S., I stated that although we lived under two very different systems, I would work to normalize relations between our two countries. The highlight for me, and certainly for him, was my singling out my old Sandwich Township High School debate coach, Carl Thokey, who, with his wife had made the trip to Washington to be present at my swearing in. I said that without him I could never have stood where I did now. Carl Thokey has assured me innumerable times since that ceremony that it was the highlight of his life.

The announcement of my appointment to Budapest received some favorable comment from the July 21, 1969 issue of *Newsweek*. Calling Nixon's appointments a "mixed bag," *Newsweek* wrote, "... there has been applause for the selection of Malcolm Toon as Beam's replacement in Prague and for Alfred Puhan as envoy to Hungary." My confirmation by the Senate Foreign Relations Committee was perfunctory and I was now ambassador extraordinary and plenipotentiary of the United States. I had reached the top rung of my service, some twenty-seven years after starting as a part-time civil service employee at GS-7.

There was an ugly incident before I left my post in Washington. Some two or three years earlier I had hired a foreign service officer upon the recommendation of the officer who was vacating a job in the Office of German Affairs. I read his bio, which showed a strong educational background—if I'm not mistaken, he had been a Rhodes scholar. I was struck by the fact that he had been at one time or another in all three of our military services. In spite of this background, he had only had two brief assignments abroad: one in Germany, for Russian language training, the second a brief tour in Moscow. The interview with him showed him to be a pleasant, intelligent officer, who for reasons that became evident only later had been passed over for promotion. I should have been warned by this, but I needed another hand in my busy office, and took him on. Not long after he had taken on his assignment, he told me that it was the most rewarding one he had yet had.

His performance was mediocre. In meetings he was articulate. He demonstrated a kind of fanaticism in situations where objectivity was called for. There were unaccounted for absences from the office. To make a long story short, when it was rating time, an annual procedure, my deputy who, upon my elevation to deputy assistant secretary, became chief of the Office of German Affairs, gave the officer a rating that was fair and accurate. As reviewing officer I realized that the report would, however, end the officer's career for he had served in a class where one more failure to be promoted would end his career as an FSO. I spoke to my former deputy about this, and while I agreed with his findings, asked him if he could not soften some of his harsher criticism of the officer. This he did, reluctantly. When I showed the rated officer his report he took exception to it which I noted. I suggested to him that he consider finding another job that did not require him to be an FSO. I mentioned a friend in the White House whom he might see, also AID, and offered to call a former colleague who was now engaged in private business. When I spoke to this former colleague, he said that he wouldn't touch the officer in question with a ten-foot pole.

I learned from the secretary of state that this officer had requested an interview with him—the secretary had no idea who he was—and had leveled all kinds of charges against me, including the assertion that I was preparing "to give away Berlin." There was more than a mere hint that my deputy and I were communists. The secretary (I learned about this not from him directly), who had known me for five years as a loyal co-worker, thought the disgruntled officer was off his rocker. However, in order to assure fairness, he appointed a board of two distinguished former ambassadors to investigate his charges. They found them absurd. That should have settled the matter. But not with this zealot.

When, as expected, he was passed over once again for promotion, he was selected out of the foreign service. Employment was found for him in the Department of Defense. There he was shortly fired by the very able future career ambassador, Lawrence Eagleburger. With the apparent support of the John Birch Society and an extremely right-wing congressman, he sought to plead a case against virtually everyone who had ever supervised him. In Budapest at the time, I received yards of testimony by this man, most of it sheer nonsense. At one point I was alerted by the director general of the foreign service that I should be prepared to return to Washington. When I replied at once that I was ready, just name the day, I never heard any more about the case.

This pathetic man—although no longer an FSO and by now known to all and sundry as someone bordering on the edge of paranoia, still managed to stand as a candidate for the directorship of the Foreign Service Association, the closest thing to a union that the foreign service has. In a hard-fought election, in which the principal candidates cut each other down he, to the astonishment of all who knew him, won. There followed a period in which the board of the Foreign Service Association found itself voting twelve to one or whatever the number of board members was, against the new president. There were reportedly some heated sessions, during one of which one of the older members of the board, fed up with the rantings of the director, hurled a water pitcher at him. Apparently it was a near miss. He was voted out of office and disappeared into the woodwork. It was a case of bad judgment on my part in hiring this man for a job in the Office of German Affairs. Overall, the failure on the part of a number of officers, with some notable exceptions, to stand up to this man was part of the legacy the late senator from Wisconsin, Joseph McCarthy, had left in officialdom.

# *Budapest*

BUDAPEST! What a joy it was to contemplate my future! I knew, of course, that I faced an uphill battle. It was difficult to imagine to what depths relations between the United States and Hungary had sunk. There were reasons for this. In 1948 we resented bitterly the takeover of Hungary by the Soviets and our ejection as one of the four powers there. There followed some awful years for the Hungarians—the Rakoczi years, harassment of an American businessman, a shooting down of a U.S. plane, and the arrest of Jozsef Cardinal Mindszenty in 1948, with the subsequent sham trial, after which the cardinal was sentenced to life imprisonment. A harassing move by the communist government inevitably resulted in retaliation by us. Thus it was that diplomatic relations between this little land-locked country in Central Europe and the United States could best be described as barely existing—but no more. Our legation in Budapest became little more than just the home in which Cardinal Mindszenty dwelt. This was not a pleasant prospect for a novice ambassador, but it certainly was a challenge.

Once again,—and this time for the last time, we crossed the Atlantic on the SS *United States*. We left New York on May 28, 1969 and arrived in LeHavre, France, on June 2. We traveled in our own little yellow Dodge Dart via Paris and Stuttgart to Vienna. From a hotel window I had a glimpse of our official car, a white Lincoln Continental, with a U.S. flag flapping merrily in the breeze.

Our stay in Budapest began on a lovely day in June. When I presented my credentials to the president of the People's Republic, Pal Losonczi, I sensed a warm, cordial atmosphere. My greatest concern before reviewing the honor guard drawn up before the Parliament building was that I would not remember the Hungarian for "Good day, soldiers!" I wrote *Jo Napot Katonak* on the palm of my left hand and came through with flying colors.

The Hungarian press headlined my arrival with "New United States Ambassador vows to work for better US-Hungary ties."

We settled down to work at once. Our first Fourth of July party—there were to be four more—was attended by some six hundred people, most of them Hungarians. Our guests on the beautifully manicured lawn of the ambassador's residence were startled to hear me propose a toast to the president of Hungary and the Hungarian people. The Soviet ambassador was perplexed to hear a capitalist toast a communist head of state. Then I asked my guests to raise their glasses to my president, President Nixon, and they did. Our guests stayed on to watch an Apollo film outdoors. It was a great day.

I asked for and got an appointment with the deputy foreign minister of the Hungarian government, Bela Szilagyi, a distinguished archeologist. We agreed on some thirty points on which we would work toward normalization of our relations. As early as August of 1969, two months after my arrival, we reached agreement on some

176

four small matters, leading the *New York Times* of August 17, 1969, to write:

> Viewed literally, the new agreement between the United States and Hungary appears modest indeed. . . . but in diplomacy the symbolism of an action is often more important than the precise details of the development. What this agreement symbolizes above all is a desire in both Washington and Budapest to improve relations, a desire whose immediate concrete embodiment is the small step now taken. And it has been possible to take this move forward despite the recent publicized Soviet warnings against building bridges between the United States and the nations of Eastern Europe. It is a good beginning for Washington's new Ambassador to Budapest, Alfred Puhan.

But I learned very quickly that all was not going to be peaches and cream. I suffered my first setback in September. There arrived in my office a telegram from Washington—"Eyes Only Ambassador"—asking me to get the Hungarians to invite the American astronauts to visit Budapest on their worldwide swing. When I noticed that Budapest was the only Eastern European post to which this request was made, I knew at once that without a stop in Moscow or at least Warsaw, the Hungarians could not comply—the Soviets would never permit it. I said as much in a cable to Washington and asked that another Eastern European country be added to the itinerary. Back came the curt reply, drafted no doubt by one of the minions on the National Security Council, that the itinerary was fixed and could not be changed. This sounded rather arch.

I had no choice but to repair to the foreign office and, putting the best possible light on the invitation, asked the deputy foreign minister to consider it. His first question—I had anticipated it—was what other Eastern European countries would be visited. I said none. He smiled and said that, of course, he could not make that decision, that he would have to put the matter before his superiors.

A day later he called me back. He was visibly upset, his face red. Now the Hungarians made a mistake. Instead of calling me in and telling me quietly that I would understand their inability to comply with our request, the deputy foreign minister had a note—in English, unfortunately. Unfortunately, because the Hungarian translator had apparently and undoubtedly inadvertently chosen the worst possible meaning of the Hungarian words. The rejection was offensive—I said as much—and denied the charge that the astronaut trip was a propaganda ploy, which, of course, it was.

I sent the Hungarian rejection to Washington, and followed it up with a reasoned analysis, avoiding meticulously any "I told you sos," and ending with the hope that this incident—so understandable, given the Soviet envy of our U.S. feat and Hungarian subjection to Soviet will would not stop us from trying to improve our relations.

Washington was silent. I received a short note from the director of the Eastern European section in Washington, my working contact at State, saying in effect, "Sorry, Al, we can't help you. Of course, you were right!" There followed a cordial but cool letter from the number two man in the State Department, Eliott Richardson, who knew me well, stating that the White House was annoyed by the Hungarian reply, and I was, until further notice, in effect to have no contact with the Hungarian government. Some of my staff in the embassy feared my short career was at an end. I did not think so.

The temporary end to our negotiations gave me and my wife, as well as our second daughter, who had joined us by now, the opportunity to become better acquainted with this ancient land in the heart of Europe. Not larger than our state of Kentucky, it was easy to traverse east, west, north and south.

My Hungarian was limited to a few expressions, but my German served me in good stead. I talked with factory managers, teachers, priests, businessmen, and farmers everywhere, and got a feel of the country. There was an amusing incident during these travels of ours.

With faithful Jeno, our Hungarian chauffeur, at the wheel of the white Lincoln, we visited Vezsprem, a charming town in southwestern Hungary. After leaving the car and Jeno in the market place, my wife, my daughter, and I visited the old town, stopping off at two churches—it was Sunday—where masses were being said. Upon returning to the car, we found a huge crowd admiring the white American automobile with the United States flag. I heard nothing but compliments. On a visit the next day to the foreign office, I told the deputy foreign minister that I had apparently visited a town that was off limits to United States diplomats, something I had not known before going there. He asked, "And what happened?"

I replied, "Nothing."

He smiled and said, "Well, that is too bad!"

Two weeks later, Mr. Szilagyi called me in to say that in view of my interest in his country, his government was lifting unilaterally all restrictions on my movements in Hungary and that I was free to cross any Hungarian border. When I reported this to Washington, the State Department reciprocated and offered the same privileges to all the Eastern European ambassadors in Washington, some of whom used the privilege.

One of our favorite spots in Hungary was Marton-vasar, some thirty kilometers from Budapest. We made good friends with Dr. Rajki, a noted geneticist, whose farm also produced the best milk in Hungary. On one of our trips to see the ruins of a castle in Hungary, my wife and I went on foot up to the castle. Upon our return to the car, we saw a young Hungarian couple near the car. The young man was trying to take a picture of his friend against the background of the white Lincoln and the fluttering American flag. To his chagrin, he was out of film. I offered to take some pictures of them with my camera, which they accepted readily. Not only did the young lady pose against the car, but also behind the wheel! I told them I would have my Hungarian chauffeur mail the pictures to them, in order to avoid any possible difficulty over receiving mail from the American ambassador. The pictures turned out great, and I am certain are now in a Hungarian album.

We pursued our interests in music, developed in Vienna years before, by going to the opera. The performances may not have been as good as the operas in Vienna, but certainly were as enjoyable.

We took a vacation at the end of August, driving our Dodge Dart to Bavaria and Italy, with Venice as the high spot of our itinerary. I participated in a gaming exercise in Garmisch-Partenkirchen, while my wife flew home to attend the funeral of her father. Glenn Seaborg, then chairman of the Atomic Energy Commission, was a surprise visitor in Budapest, as was Edgar Bergen. We shared our first Thanksgiving dinner with five marines, the first to appear in Budapest in years. It was the result of an agreement I had reached with the foreign office. While I was aware that five young, single men in a communist country presented the possibility of mischief, their taking over the patroling of the embassy at night, a task usually performed by embassy officers hitherto, it was a great relief for my small staff of twenty-five Americans. By keeping a sharp eye on the marines, we experienced no trouble and were greatly pleased with their performance.

At Christmas time 1969 we gave the first of our Christmas parties for both the American and Hungarian staff. The latter had tears in their eyes as they sang ancient carols and received their small gifts.

Among our guests was an interesting woman, Kitty Hoffman, a teacher from Baltimore. Unlike the rest of the Americans, she could not leave Budapest for she was, in effect, under house arrest. Her predicament arose from an automobile accident in which she was unhappily involved. She was driving a rented car with the ex-wife of a U.S. senator as passenger toward Vienna. Somewhere between Budapest and the border, she crossed the oncoming lane of traffic to buy gas at one of the then few gas stations. A motorcyclist rounding a curve at great speed smashed into Kitty's car and was killed instantly.

We learned of the detainment of the two women from an anonymous caller. I dispatched our vice consul to the town where they were being held. Although we had no consular convention with Hungary at the time, the Hungarian authorities released the two women to us—the passenger was allowed to continue her trip home—but Kitty had to stand trial.

Under Hungarian law, Kitty was guilty of second degree murder. Her trial, attended by a prominent lawyer from Baltimore, resulted in a stiff seven-year sentence. When the American lawyer asked me to intervene, I told him to wait and see how the appeal would come out. The result was a reduction of her sentence by three years.

At this point, without instructions from Washington, I went to the foreign office to plead the case of Kitty Hoffman, noting that her jailing would serve no useful purpose, that we could help the widow of the killed motorcyclist, and that her jailing would not be helpful in our mutual desire to improve relations between our two countries. My plea was apparently persuasive. Two weeks later I was informed that the Hungarian government would pardon her but that she would have to serve a token sentence of four or six weeks. At this point I lost my aplomb and said that the Hungarians would negate their kind action with this silly sentence. In Washington, the only thing that would be remembered was her jailing, even for a short time. Once again, reconsideration, and then I was told Kitty was free but her release should not be reported in the American press. I threw up my hands and said that I had absolutely no power whatsoever—unlike the Hungarian government and its tightly controlled press—to tell the American press what to write and what not to write.

Kitty Hoffman arrived in Baltimore, with the Baltimore papers on strike! To my knowledge, nothing appeared in U.S. papers. I am not sure but that the Hungarian officials did not believe my disclaimer about our power over the press.

We were happy to see Kitty Hoffman free. She had been a delightful guest and, indeed, had become a kind of member of the embassy. More importantly there was something I did not know at first—that she was well known to certain high U.S. government officials. In any event I received a congratulatory message from Washington. Even more important, I received a request to renew our quest of improving U.S.-Hungarian relations.

Evidence of the thaw in our relations was a movie

we were permitted to show in a public place. The Hungarian Science Museum displayed a moon rock brought to earth by Neil Armstrong. The prime minister attended the opening of the American Pavilion at the Trade Fair. David Broder wrote in the *New York Times* that the US and Hungary were pleased by improving relations.

In June of 1970 I realized a dream that I never thought would come true. With my wife and Fred, my son who had joined us by now, and with Jeno at the wheel, we drove across Czechoslovakia and Poland, stopping in Cracow and Warsaw. Our goal was the place of my birth, Marienburg, on the former East-West Prussian border, now a Polish city named Malbork.

Leaving Warsaw, I felt a distinct mounting tension as we drove toward what used to be East Prussia. Although a quarter of a century had passed since the Poles were awarded this former German land, the demarcation was still very clear—the former German villages and towns with their bright red brick walls and tile roofs, although somewhat run down, looked more substantial than the old Poland we left behind. When we got too close to the Russian border near Koenigsberg (now Kaliningrad), we were stopped by Polish police. They were nonplussed to find an American ambassador in a white Lincoln, chauffeured by a Hungarian, and none of whom spoke Polish! Our documents, however, were in order, and we were turned in the direction of Gdansk, the former Danzig. I saw Marienburg earlier than I had expected. Of the bridge we used to cross with our smuggled goods, only a few piles remained. The Nogat River seemed much smaller than I remembered it. The Poles have faithfully restored the Teutonic Knights castle, and there remains a gate of the old wall at the opposite end of the town. In between, the Poles have built the typically unattractive communist apartment houses. They were just so many gray cement boxes, totally lacking grace and charm.

We toured the old castle, and I remembered much of it still after all these years. We stayed in the old Grand Hotel in Sopot, the once-famous German resort of Zoppot. Danzig has been carefully restored—the Neptune fountain, the Artushof, the Zeughaus were still there.

But I wanted to see Halbstadt (Half City) where I had spent the years of my youth in the Germany I remembered best. I never saw Halbstadt! It was spring, and the dikes that contained the Nogat River in flood time, which had been cut by German troops in an effort to stop the advancing Russians, had never been repaired. We tried every approach to this little village of my youth only to find our Lincoln in water hubcap deep. It was a disappointment.

Visitors were now more frequent in Budapest. Lionel Hampton brought his band, which brought the house down in the downtown theater. Senator Ellender stayed with us at the ambassador's residence, as did Congressman Vanik and party and Congressman Reuss. I saw to it that my staff got out to Vienna monthly, just to be even briefly in a noncommunist world. We made it perhaps every three months, frequently the guest of the generous United States ambassador to Austria, John Humes.

In 1971 we had home leave to be present at the wedding of our second daughter, Faxie, to her high school sweetheart, now an Annapolis graduate. Our older daughter had married some four years earlier, and she and her husband spent only a brief but enjoyable visit with us in Budapest.

The highlight of the year of 1971, however, was the departure from the embassy of Jozsef Cardinal Mindszenty. His story deserves a special chapter.

# The Mindszenty Story:
# 1969–1971

$M$Y interest in Jozsef Cardinal Mindszenty grew rapidly when I learned early in 1969 that I would be designated as ambassador to Hungary. Like other officials of the State Department I had, of course, been aware of his presence in the American embassy since 1956. I recall very vividly his entry on November 4, 1956, when Russian tanks finally put down the revolution, which came close to freeing Hungary. I had met him twice before coming here in 1969. The first time, in 1960, was while I was executive director of the European Bureau of the State Department, and arrived in Budapest from Moscow. I was impressed on that occasion by the almost total isolation in which he was kept, even from official visitors from the United States. The minister of the legation at that time was visibly upset when he learned that his deputy had invited me to attend the Sunday mass of the cardinal. The occasion turned out to be a moving one, with the cardinal preaching a fiery political sermon.

The following year, in 1961, I actually met Cardinal Mindszenty and had a rather superficial conversation with him.

During my preparations for my assignment as ambassador to Budapest, I found remarkably little in the official records about him. There was the account of his entry into the embassy in 1956. For the next thirteen years there was actually very little. It was clear that he lived the life of a hermit in the ambassador's office where he had been installed upon his arrival on November 4, 1956. His contact was mainly with the members of the American legation, which had been raised to an embassy in 1967. He saw very few outsiders: these included a very few high-ranking members of the executive branch of the government, none or virtually no members of the legislative, and no private persons. He was visited on the average of once or twice a year by the cardinal of Vienna, Cardinal Koenig. These visits seem to have served no great purpose other than to convince Koenig that Mindszenty was a stubborn old man who was totally out of step with the times. He saw no Hungarians other than close relatives on rare occasions and a Hungarian priest, who heard his confession. His contacts with the outside world were channeled by way of the State Department to the Apostolic Nuncio in Washington who, if he regarded it an appropriate message, forwarded it to the Vatican. Most of the messages concerned greetings on commemorative occasions.

In Washington I found a man who acted as the "housekeeper" of the cardinal and who simultaneously was entrusted with the mysterious crown of Saint Stephen. The official position of the United States government, as told to me during my briefings, was that the cardinal in our embassy was no concern of ours. He was strictly the problem of the government of Hungary and the Vatican, and that we were silent bystanders who had granted him asylum. The attitude in Washington during those days of preparation for my ambassadorship in Budapest toward Cardinal Mindszenty was simply that every chief of mission had to accommodate himself to the presence of this high-ranking prelate of the Roman Catholic Church. Too much time had passed to leave much hope that he would ever leave. His demands for total rehabilitation and the equally stubborn refusal on the part of the Hungarian government to grant these terms, plus the lackadaisical attitude of the Vatican and our own willingness to have him remain, appeared to exclude any possibility of a solution. The last time there had been a flare-up over his presence had been in 1967, when my predecessor, Martin J. Hillenbrand, was appointed as the first ambassador to Hungary. The cardinal on that occasion threatened to walk out of the embassy into the arms of the Hungarian police. Apparently because of fears that there would be repercussions at home, repercussions which would be felt by certain members of Congress as well as the executive branch, the Vatican was persuaded to send Cardinal Koenig to Budapest and plead with Cardinal Mindszenty to remain in his asylum. Mindszenty, having scored his point, remained and Hillenbrand arrived as the first ambassador.

When I came to Budapest in June of 1969 I established a pattern of relations with him, which did not noticeably differ from that of my predecessors. I would, however, seldom go to see him and met him more frequently on neutral ground, that is, at a conference room used by the embassy officers, or in my own office. I found him, from the beginning, cool and correct in his attitude toward me. I saw him for rather lengthy talks on the average of once a month. During these talks, lasting anywhere from one to two hours, he preferred to dwell on the past misfortunes of his native land. It was during my very first meeting with him that he raised the Treaty of

Trianon of 1920, as he was to do so many times in the months and years that followed. By this treaty, for which he held Woodrow Wilson primarily responsible, Hungary, because of ending up on the losing side at the end of World War I, lost almost two-thirds of her lands to her neighbors. Mindszenty as a strong Hungarian nationalist could never forgive the authors of this treaty for their actions, and I fear it colored his attitude toward the United States, whose hospitality he accepted and, formally at least, appreciated. Much of his conversation dwelt with the evils of communism and his fears of a total takeover by the communists. He told me on one occasion that the last strong opponent of communism had been Konrad Adenauer, the first postwar chancellor of the Federal Republic of Germany. He had no faith in the men who were running the post-World War II governments of Western Europe and he thought generally that the United States' leadership was naive.

Mindszenty's world, as disclosed in these conversations, consisted largely of his own impressions of Rakocsi Hungary plus an avid reading of the Hungarian refugee press, which he received regularly from the United States. To be sure, he scanned the *Neue Zuercher Zeitung* and *Die Presse* as well as the Paris edition of the *Herald Tribune*. However, from the articles he called to my attention or that of other embassy officers, it was clear that he read what he wanted to read, and read only those articles that did not change his conception of the world in which we live. Although he had been provided with a radio, he used it chiefly to "jam" his conversations with others in his office. He turned down an offer of a TV set. Indeed, he seldom glanced out at the square below his windows. He once told me when I said that his room was rather dark that he preferred that kind of darkness to looking out upon the Soviet memorial in *Szabadsag Ter* (Freedom Square). Lacking the stimulus of real dialogue and contact with the outside world, he was either unaware of, or refused to believe that great changes were taking place, even in Hungary. He was wont to dismiss the beneficial effect of greater contact the Hungarians had with foreigners as a result of the rapidly increasing number of tourists in Hungary, with the comment that such tourism only aided communism in extinguishing Christendom.

The cardinal in these earlier conversations with me refused to be led into a discussion of his future. Any hint on my part regarding his health or possible difficulties that might arise was met with silence. It became clear to me that he had become accustomed to his asylum in the American embassy. In fact, the embassy had become home to him. While a cardinal in name, he was in fact acting out the role of a small village priest who had a tiny, constantly changing, Sunday congregation. He was satisfied with the food provided him by two Hungarian cooks in the coffee shop in the embassy basement. He used his fifteen-minute walks at 5:30 each afternoon in the little enclosed courtyard of the embassy for the ventilation of his views to officers who frequently were not terribly interested or were not too well informed regarding the subject matter he was talking about.

Although he had apparently suffered from tuberculosis some four years before I arrived, his health for a man his age was generally good. There were days, particularly during the hot days of July and August, when he seemed to sag and show the effects of his age. But he always seemed to bounce back rather quickly. His voice was firm and his eyes were clear. This was the Mindszenty I found when I came here and whom I had gotten to know better during the first year of my stay in Budapest.

The Hungarian government was silent on Cardinal Mindszenty when I first arrived here. I noted that when Deputy Foreign Minister Bela Szilagyi and I devised an agenda of some thirty items that called for a solution in order to bring about a normalization of our relations, he did not suggest the inclusion of Cardinal Mindszenty. He did ask for the inclusion of the crown of St. Stephen but never mentioned the name of the cardinal or his presence in the American embassy. I recall the very first time I ever mentioned the cardinal's name to Hungarian officialdom. It came about in the following manner: we had agreed that in our discussions of problems, which we hoped to solve in order to normalize relations between the United States and Hungary we would have a note taker on each side. The Hungarians, to be sure, had three or four, and I invariably took the brilliant young economic officer, Herbert Wilgis. There came a time in August of 1969 when Mr. Wilgis was out of the country as was my deputy chief of mission, the political officer was ill with a strep throat, and the administrative officer had just learned of the death of her closest relative in the United States, causing her to depart. I went to my meeting with Mr. Szilagyi alone. He queried me regarding the absence of my note taker. I responded simply that my embassy was so small I had no one left to accompany me, and the only advisor I could have taken along, the Hungarian government would not have permitted me to bring. There was a momentary pause in the conversation, some consternation, and then uproarious laughter! Thus began my dialogue with the Hungarians about Cardinal Mindszenty.

The problem, as it appeared to me in 1969, was to

bring about a change in three policies before the Cardinal himself could be tackled on a change of venue. The first was to convince the Hungarians that it was in their interest to see the cardinal depart from the American embassy. The second was to get the State Department to change its long-held position that this particular problem was no concern of ours, for its assistance would be required in getting the Vatican to act. The third was to change the noncommittal policy of the Vatican and get it to put greater steam behind the effort to move Mindszenty out of the embassy. It seemed quite clear to me right from the outset that he probably could not remain in Hungary if he left the embassy, but I did think it was not impossible to get him moved out of the country. It was clear to my advisors and myself that Mindszenty himself would probably not move except if virtually ordered to do so by the pope. He had always stressed his obedience to the head of the Roman Catholic Church and there was no reason to doubt that if the Vatican were prepared to order him out he would conceivably procrastinate but would eventually obey.

The first task, it seemed to me, was to produce a change in the attitude of the Hungarian government. Certain factors in the international political situation seemed to work in our favor. Janos Kadar was now in his thirteenth year as leader of the Hungarian Communist Party. In 1968 he had embarked upon a far-reaching economic program that was designed to make Hungary, in two or three years, economically speaking, the most advanced of the Eastern Europe states. Kadar had permitted the process of liberalization to take place, so that there was greater freedom for the Hungarian people. Mindszenty, however, was always dismissed, as pointed out earlier, as not a factor in any of this move toward liberalization.

It was by the process of quiet conversations with members of the Hungarian Foreign Office initially, and later with people beyond that ministry, that we planted the advantages of a Mindszenty departure from Hungary. I recall a conversation with the vice-president of the country, Beresztoczy, himself an excommunicated priest, during which I noted that the death of Mindszenty in the American embassy would certainly lead to a total rehash of the events of 1948, 1949, and 1956 and would not redound to the credit of the Hungarian government. I enlisted at various times the aid of my diplomatic colleagues, notably the French, Swiss and Austrian ambassadors, who all acted independently, if sporadically, to bring about a change in the Hungarian attitude.

I knew that progress had been made when I was told by one of my best contacts in the Hungarian Foreign Office to raise the subject of Mindszenty's future with Janos Kadar, with whom an appointment had been set up for me. Since Hungarian officials are not known to act on their own initiative, it was clear that Kadar had had a change of mind and was interested in a solution to the Mindszenty problem. My meeting with him did not materialize at that time because of events elsewhere that made a meeting of the American ambassador with Kadar undesirable from his point of view. I was told on another occasion that if the American ambassador wished to take Mindszenty in his car and speed him across the Hungarian border, no one would stop him. There were other indications. It was easier to discuss the Mindszenty case. There were even occasional inquiries on the part of Hungarian officials regarding his health and his current state of mind. By the fall of 1970 I had the impression that the

Hungarian side at least would conceivably entertain new talks concerning the cardinal.

The American side remained consistent in its views. From communications, private letters, and conversations with officials from Washington, I got the impression that we had become so accustomed to the cardinal's living with us that a change in his status was inconceivable. I was confirmed in this view by my visit to Washington in March of 1970, almost a year after I had come to Budapest. The problem, therefore, was to shake Washington out of this state of mind and get it to move.

In general, relations between our two countries had improved somewhat. It could be said at the beginning of 1971 that relations between the largest and most powerful member of NATO and little Hungary, securely locked in the Warsaw Pact, with a leadership totally subservient to Moscow in international matters, were normal. Small advances had been made on a number of issues and, while there were ups and downs created as the result of tensions between the United States and the U.S.S.R., which were immediately reflected in our relations with Hungary, relations on the whole were developing in a satisfactory fashion.

It was in January of 1971, eight months before the cardinal's departure from the embassy, that we made the move to get Washington off the dime. I noted in a communication the problems that appeared to be in the offing for us with a man who would soon be in his eightieth year. I urged that we stir the Vatican up, saying that we should not just let things go on as they had gone on for years, that we owed it to the cardinal, as well as to history that we change from our passive attitude toward one of action. We introduced a note of urgency into the first message. It is curious, in retrospect that, this message of

January 13, 1971, was never formally answered. There followed some correspondence with State Department officials in which the urgency of the first message was reiterated and a reaction from the department that the sense of urgency was making itself felt in Washington.

There arose at this time the subject of the cardinal's memoirs. It was known that the cardinal was working on his memoirs. No one had seen them although bits and pieces had, at times, been available to the wife of an officer or a secretary for transcription. The cardinal also had, at various times, asked for church chronicles, which he explained he needed for his memoirs. It became clear to my closest advisor, my deputy chief of mission, and to me that these memoirs would play a powerful role if there were to be any change brought about in his asylum.

The cardinal had asked the president of the United States for permission to have his memoirs edited in Vienna by a former parish priest of his who was at the time in South Bend, Indiana. The reply to this letter was an oral one given by the State Department to the embassy to communicate to him, to the effect that his request was impossible to comply with since there was a danger of a leak of premature publication while the cardinal was still in the American embassy.

In the meantime, the cardinal had become aware of some press publicity regarding a possible return of the Crown of Saint Stephen to the Hungarian government. He was greatly upset by this news and was only partly assured by an oral assurance that there was no intention to transfer this Hungarian national treasure to the Hungarians at this point. A word here about the Crown of St. Stephen. This revered relic, symbol of Hungarian nationalism, was said to have been given to the Hungarian King Istvan by Pope Sylvester in the tenth century. It is difficult to believe, with all the invasions of Hungary during the nearly one thousand years since that time, that the Crown of St. Stephen could have survived. But legend or fact, it appeared at various times in history and was hidden from marauders until the Russians entered Hungary in 1944. At that time, Hungarian soldiers fearing that the Russians would steal this holy relic, took the Crown, along with some other relics, on their flight westward. They surrendered to American troops near Salzburg, who took the sacred symbol of Hungarian nationalism into their possession. When the war ended in 1945, the plan was to return the Crown to Budapest. However, the years passed rapidly and by 1948 no American wanted to return the Crown. For years it reposed in West Germany. When the Federal Republic of Germany was proclaimed, the Crown was moved to Fort Knox, Kentucky, rarely seen by anyone. Since relations between the United States and Hungary were so poor, no effort was made to return it. Moreover, the Hungarian communist government was reluctant to raise this symbol of Hungarian nationalism. But it was never forgotten by the Hungarians.

Unbeknownst to me, the State Department had apparently started some wheels in motion to begin a dialogue with the Vatican regarding the cardinal's future. I had, at one time, suggested taking up this matter with the president's new personal representative to the Vatican, Henry Cabot Lodge, whom I had known when he was ambassador to Germany and I was deputy assistant secretary of state in Washington. From a letter from a member of ambassador Lodge's staff in Rome, I learned that obviously the department was discussing the cardinal with the Vatican.

In the meantime, the Hungarian foreign minister,

Janos Peter, visited Rome. On April 16, 1971 he was received for forty-five minutes by the pope. Although there were denials that Mindszenty had been discussed, Kadar, in an interview a few days later on April 20, said "We would like to further the settlement of certain questions." He appeared to ask for an initiative on Cardinal Mindszenty.

We used the occasion of the medical officer's visit from Vienna, at this time in April and his regular examination of the cardinal, to once again impress upon the state department some urgency in moving with the Vatican. By April 20 the department, in a cautiously worded letter, gave a hint that: "We, too, may try to stir the Vatican to action." The situation began to look a little more hopeful, at least as far as these primary stages were concerned. Still in April I learned from a member of Ambassador Lodge's staff that officials in the Vatican were showing a heightened interest in the Mindszenty case. One of these officials came up with what was a most imaginative idea. This was to find a Hungarian churchman in whom Cardinal Mindszenty had confidence to convince him that his departure would be in the best interests of all concerned. I wrote this official that I regarded this suggestion as imaginative and one that broke new ground. To be sure, it would not be easy to find such a churchman, since the cardinal generally had a rather low opinion of the Catholic clergy in Hungary. At the same time, while taking kindly to the suggestion, we did not fail to point out that if anything was going to succeed in moving the cardinal, it would have to be a request from the pope himself. We also took the occasion to stress the importance of the memoirs to the cardinal.

On the subject of the memoirs, we had been led to believe that the Vatican was very cool regarding their publication. From the known views of the cardinal on various matters in which the Vatican had an interest, it was understandable. It was thus necessary to convince the Vatican that while the publication of the memoirs would have rough spots for all of us, we could live with them.

In retrospect, this letter from a member of Ambassador Lodge's staff in Rome was a turning point. It was the first time that we had a channel from Budapest to Rome. In the past, it will be recalled, all messages concerning the cardinal and the Vatican had to be channeled through the State Department to the Apostolic Delegate in Washington, who presumably passed the information on to the Vatican. I had learned during my stay in Washington in March of 1970 that this channel was not terribly effective as far as moving the Vatican was concerned. But the letter from Rome gave promise of new possibilities. It also shed light on activities carried on by the Vatican as the result, presumably in part at least, of Washington intercession.

In the meantime, on May 11, 1971, I met with Cardinal Mindszenty prior to my departure on May 14 for consultations. He appeared anxious to have a talk with me. He wanted to discuss his memoirs. He noted the importance of these memoirs to him and his place in history. He repeated his request, which he had made in writing earlier, that they be sent to Vienna, where Monsignor Szabo, his former parish priest now living in South Bend, Indiana, could read them and correct them. I knew at the time of my conversation with him that his request was bound to be fruitless and I told him so. Nonetheless, I said I would check on the subject when I went to Washington. I used this occasion, however, to ask the cardinal if he had ever considered other ways in accomplishing his objective, that is, the publication of his memoirs. I reminded him of Kadar's recent invitation for an initiative on the cardinal. I reminded him further that Foreign Minister Peter had just had a meeting with the pope. I told him I didn't want him to misunderstand me. I said it was obviously a matter he would have to decide for himself, and that if he wanted to stay here until he died, that would be acceptable to us. I concluded by telling him that if he wanted his memoirs published, he would have to be in a position to supervise that project. Mindszenty did not react directly to my remarks, but listened carefully to what I told him. I told him I would see him again after my return from Washington.

Two days later I met with Hungarian Foreign Minister Janos Peter. He raised the subject of Cardinal Mindszenty. Without disclosing what the pope had said during his conversation with him in Rome, he nonetheless gave me to understand that the Vatican was interested in a solution, and that the government of Hungary was prepared for a real solution. I was struck by the complete change in the Hungarian position by his remarks that the cardinal's presence in the Embassy was a problem for Hungary, as well as for the Vatican, and for the American embassy. The foreign minister informed me that he expected Vatican officials in the very near future to try to bring about a solution of the Mindszenty problem. He told me that the Hungarians would insist, in letting Mindszenty depart Hungary, that the cardinal should not become a tool in a new cold war against Hungary.

On the evening of the same day that I saw Peter I learned from the French ambassador that there was indeed work going on on the part of Vatican officials hoping to find a solution to the Mindszenty case. With this information fresh in mind, I left on May 14 for home.

While my consultations were not to take place until June 13, in fact I met with three officers of the Department of State while passing through Washington on May 17. I was able to give these officials some useful insights in the Mindszenty problem, which apparently led them to greater activity in urging the Vatican to encourage Mindszenty to depart his native land.

For nearly a month I was practically out of touch with the situation surrounding the cardinal. Upon my arrival in Washington for consultation I learned that Ambassador Lodge was very much in the picture. I also learned that a delegation from Rome, led by Monsignor Cheli, would be arriving in the latter half of June to consult with the Hungarian government as well as with the Cardinal. Cardinal Koenig from Vienna would introduce the Vatican negotiators to Cardinal Mindszenty. The Department of State was now very effective in instructing our embassy in Rome and Ambassador Lodge on how to deal with the Vatican. When I heard that Cardinal Koenig would arrive in Budapest I sent a letter, which I asked my chargé d'affaires to deliver to him upon his arrival. It stressed the significance of this effort. I noted that I greatly feared that if we failed this time we might not have another opportunity. I regretted my absence from Budapest at this time and hoped that we would all be prudent in dealing discreetly with this subject and wished him all the success in his mission.

The cardinal from Vienna called on the cardinal on June 23. The meeting, like so many between these two, was somewhat perfunctory. His call was followed up by a visit of Monsignor Cheli and Monsignor Zagon for three meetings with Cardinal Mindszenty on June 25, 26, and 27.

A word is necessary here about a remarkable man,

who was more responsible for changing the cardinal's mind than perhaps anyone else, although of course he could never have done it without the assistance of the pope. He is Monsignor Zagon, a tall, white-haired Hungarian churchman, a former priest of Cardinal Mindszenty's diocese who left Hungary in 1948. Cardinal Mindszenty had been his hero. He accepted, with mixed feelings, the task of persuading Mindszenty to leave Hungary. He had not been back to Hungary since he left and had been deprived of his citizenship. His sympathies were with Mindszenty. But he enjoyed the confidence of the cardinal, and as it turned out, he had the courage to continue for hours on end in talking to the cardinal.

These three meetings between Zagon and the cardinal in the last days of June of 1971 resulted first in a refusal on the part of the cardinal to sign a document that he would leave the embassy and Hungary. They also resulted in a startling reversal on his part on June 28. He wrote two letters, one to the president of the U.S., the second to the pope. He told the president that he was prepared to leave Hungary if this was considered in the best interests of his church. He asked for the president's advice.

To the pope he sent a letter, which was released in part by the Vatican after his arrival in Rome, in which the cardinal said, "I wish to spend the rest of my life in Hungary regardless of the external restrictions that await me. If, however, the passions aroused against me or other considerations of the utmost importance for the Church should make this impossible, I will take up perhaps the heaviest cross of my life and will be willing to leave my beloved fatherland, so that I may continue in exile my prayers and acts of penance in behalf of the Church of Hungary."

When I arrived in Budapest from Washington on June 28, my devoted deputy told me that the cardinal had promised to leave Budapest. He added it looked as though we were approaching the end of an era.

The next three months turned out to be the most difficult in our relations with Cardinal Mindszenty. It appeared that almost immediately after he had given his decision to the pope to leave the embassy and Hungary, he had regretted it. He spent much of his time in the ensuing three months finding obstacles to his going. I was not anxious to see him so soon after my return from consultations in Washington, for I had very little to tell him that would cheer him up or indeed, hasten the process of moving him out of the embassy. While the Vatican was casting about for a papal messenger to bring the pope's reply to Cardinal Mindszenty's letter, I was preparing myself for my first meeting with the cardinal. I knew that the subject of his memoirs would be high on the agenda.

The cardinal disclosed his state of mind to Clem Scerback, the American public affairs officer, who had taken over the functions of aide to the cardinal with the departure of Ross Titus. At one point early in July the cardinal said that the thought had struck him that with his departure he would give Janos Kadar great joy. He accused Kadar of being responsible for 2.5 million Hungarian abortions. He asked whether his departure would improve the position of the church. Then the cardinal told my deputy that he was most anxious to see me before the next round of visitors from Rome. The Vatican had decided that Cheli and Zagon would return on or about July 14. I met with the cardinal on July 12 for approximately twenty minutes. He looked tired, drawn, unshaven, and was most serious. I explained that I had purposely stayed away from him, not wishing to disturb him in his important deliberations regarding his future. I told him that there was no change on the question he had raised with me prior to my departure for Washington regarding the possibility of having his memoirs edited by an outsider in Vienna. We could not agree with this. He asked me point-blank why he had never received a written reply to his letters. This was the beginning of a period of fretting and worrying about a letter from the president. He indicated that the absence of a reply to his letter to the President meant he would be unable to give a firm reply to the representatives of the Vatican. He needed the president's views on his departure. He became quite petulant, saying that in the early days of his asylum in the American embassy, he used to receive personal letters from the president of the United States. In more recent years, however, he had failed to receive a single reply in writing. He next took off on the Vatican in a most critical manner.

I assured him he had always received replies, albeit not over the signature of the president. I repeated our preparedness for him to remain where he was and that the matter of his departure was something he would have to decide himself. Quite clearly he was seeking support of his view, at this time, that he should not leave the embassy and Hungary.

It came as a surprise to me when I received a telegraphic message on July 14 that the president had signed a letter to Cardinal Mindszenty dated July 14, in which he expressed his satisfaction in having been able to render assistance to the cardinal when his need was greatest. The president reiterated the American position that decisions about the cardinal's future were of course for him and the Vatican to make. I lost no time in presenting the text of this presidential letter to the cardinal. To me, he appeared almost disappointed in having received a letter he claimed he had wanted very badly earlier. His cryptic comment, besides a short word of thanks, was "Why so late? Why had there been no reply earlier?"

In the meantime, Monsignori Cheli and Zagon arrived for another series of meetings with the cardinal that extended over a period of three days. Cheli had two letters with him for the cardinal, one from the pope, and the other from the Vatican Secretary of State Villot. Once again Zagon did all of the negotiating with Cardinal Mindszenty. After three hard bargaining sessions Monsignor Zagon reported that the cardinal had agreed to set a date on the following day for his departure from Budapest. He posed a number of conditions, none of which seemed insurmountable. He raised his ante occasionally during these meetings, listed "conditions" that the Hungarians would have to meet in return for his departure, which were for the most part not attainable. It became apparent during these talks with Zagon that his information regarding the state of the church in Hungary was incomplete.

Zagon turned out to be a shrewd and tough negotiator who eventually pointed out to the old cardinal that his reputation in history would not be enhanced by his continued residence in the American embassy. When the cardinal had exhausted one set of conditions, he raised the question of his memoirs and their safe shipment outside of Hungary. Zagon concluded the third session of his talks by asking him if the pope could be assured that the cardinal would leave Budapest at the end of August or at the beginning of September. Mindszenty promised to agree to a date in a fourth meeting.

During this fourth meeting on July 16 the cardinal

approved a *pro memoria,* indicating his hope to leave the United States embassy in September or at the latest, in October. We had assured him via Zagon that his memoirs would be safely conveyed outside of the country and would be held in safekeeping for him until he called for them himself. It appeared at this point that the cardinal was pretty securely committed to a departure at a foreseeable date. There remained, to be sure, matters between the Vatican and the government of Hungary, but from all indications it looked as if the Hungarian government would be fairly flexible on meeting the Vatican's demands.

The Vatican negotiators left on July 16. Almost at once the cardinal began to reflect on his decision and to find ways of stalling. He hounded Scerback to get him chronicles and books on church history in Hungary, with the reminder that he would not be able to leave here until he had completed his memoirs. While the requests he made seemed rather unrelated to the present, he stressed the importance of getting these books, and left no doubt that he would not turn his memoirs over to anyone until he had completed them.

On July 21 I was received by Hungarian Foreign Minister Janos Peter. Peter was well informed regarding the activities of the Vatican representatives and the Cardinal's plans. He assured me that the Vatican proposals for certain church matters affecting the government of Hungary would be dealt with in a speedy and forthcoming manner. He stressed his conviction that the Cardinal's departure would be beneficial in our efforts to normalize United States-Hungarian relations.

Shortly thereafter the cardinal expressed satisfaction that we would find a way of getting his memoirs out of Budapest. But he had a new worry. This was the need of an assurance over the president's signature that the memoirs would be put into his hands and nobody else's except someone delegated by him after he had left Hungary. Since the request seemed to suggest suspicion of the motives of the Vatican I counseled against a presidential assurance, but asked instead that I be authorized, after due consultations with the Vatican, to assure the cardinal that his memoirs would be turned over to him or his designated agent after he had left Hungary. In the meantime, his anticipation of a second presidential letter of reassurance regarding his memoirs began to mount. He refused to ask me about this matter but used a roundabout way, through Scerback, regarding a letter from the president. News was received by telegram from the cardinal's nephew in a small village in Hungary that Mindszenty's sister had died. This came as a great blow to the cardinal, who was under considerable stress at this point anyway. It was hard to determine whether the death of his closest relative would tend to move him in the direction of Vienna and Rome or toward staying in Budapest. I sent him condolences on behalf of my government and the embassy, which he acknowledged in a brief reply. It did not take him long, however, to recover from the loss of his sister, for on July 28 he asked Scerback to compose a telegram to the president of the United States, asking him to sign a note to the effect that his memoirs would be handed over to him or his designated representative without delay or without protest.

The cardinal almost immediately harassed members of the embassy staff, particularly Scerback. He even went so far as to ask my secretary whether his telegram had in fact been sent to Washington. Some apparent ambiguity in Scerback's reply, plus his great suspicion, left the Cardinal in an increasingly agitated state of mind.

I appealed to the Department of State to immediately authorize me to guarantee to the cardinal that his memoirs would be safely conveyed out of Budapest and would be turned over to him or his designated agent after he had left Budapest. The process required considerable coordination with the Vatican, which had no objection to the course proposed by me, but it took a lot of time. The recurrence of pain in one of the cardinal's feet as a result of an earlier injury, plus a fall in the shower, the heat of August, and the stress under which he lived, caused him to be exceedingly difficult to live with. In telegram after telegram I stressed the need for an urgent reply to the cardinal. It appeared to me at one time that he was even considering once again the possibility of walking out of the embassy into the arms of the Hungarian police. In fact, he went so far as to tell Scerback at one point that if he had not made a binding commitment to the pope to leave Budapest he would now embarrass Kadar by walking out. He began to describe himself as no longer a guest in the embassy but rather a prisoner. He fretted over his accounts of the small donations he had made at various times during his stay in the past fifteen years to the poor and to charitable organizations. He made requests, which, in view of the absence of documentation, were well nigh impossible to fulfill. By the middle of August I became convinced that action one way or the other was imperative.

Finally, on August 17, I received authority to tell the Cardinal that his precious memoirs would be turned over to him or his designated agent after he had left Hungary. There remained one difference to be ironed out between myself and the department. The department wanted me to make an oral presentation; I asked for a letter signed by me in lieu of one requested by the cardinal from the president. I knew that without a letter of some sort he would never accept the guarantee. To iron out this difference required a few more days.

I must say that all of us in the embassy were relieved when the American doctor arrived from Vienna to examine the cardinal and found his ailments amenable to treatment in the embassy. At the same time, however, the correctness of the position we had taken in January that sooner or later we would be confronted with an invalided cardinal, with no place to get treatment except in Hungary itself, came true.

On August 24 I had the most painful confrontation with the cardinal of my entire relationship with him. Scerback had told him on the day before that I would like to see him at 10:00 o'clock the following morning. While he agreed on the time, he informed Scerback on the morning of August 24 that he did not feel himself qualified or prepared to talk to the ambassador without being told specifically whether or not his telegram to the president had been sent. Although Scerback had indicated to him that it had, he took the position that this was a matter for the ambassador to answer. Finally, he agreed to meet with me.

Our meeting took place in the conference room and lasted forty minutes. The cardinal, in a high state of dudgeon, drew himself up to his full height and said he would refuse to sit down because he had received no reply to his telegram to the president about his memoirs. When I suggested, calmly but firmly, to him that this was precisely why I had asked him to meet with me and asked him to sit down, he hesitated but then took a chair, probably the only time in history that a cardinal has been told by an ambassador in no uncertain terms to sit down!

Patiently I went over the ground with him on his

memoirs. I assured him that I had sent his message, requesting President Nixon's personal guaranty that his memoirs would be delivered to him or to his designated representative after he left here. I pointed out that I was in the position to give him the response of the United States government. I told him that I was acting as the president's personal representative, and that I was delivering to him a reply. I read him my reply and then gave him the letter.

The cardinal was obviously less pleased than he would have been had he received a letter from President Nixon. However, he could not in good faith refuse the assurances that I had given him. Instead, he turned with considerable bitterness to rehash the fact that he had received no reply to a letter he had sent more than a year ago. When I reminded him that I recalled this occasion, that he had in fact received an oral reply, both from an embassy officer and from myself, he spoke with great bitterness of the offense to a cardinal of the Roman Catholic Church in not receiving a reply from the president. Our meeting closed on a cool but correct note.

The problem, it was clear, was that too much time had been allowed to elapse since he had made his decision to leave and his actual departure. He had too much time to reconsider his decision and was obviously unhappy over it. I wrote a rather impatient and bitter letter to an officer on Ambassador Lodge's staff in Rome on September 1, complaining of the loss of momentum on the part of the Vatican. I pointed out in closing my letter that we had reached a historical moment where the opportunity existed to get him out of Budapest. It probably would not come again if we failed.

Rome reported that Cheli would be arriving in Budapest in early September for discussions with the government of Hungary regarding Mindszenty's departure. It was clear that Cheli had no intention of calling on the cardinal, but that he might call me. The department was once again supporting fully our actions to get moving on this matter.

Early in the month of September the postmaster general of the United States, Winton Blount, and his family arrived for a brief visit to Hungary, during which Mr. Blount saw the foreign minister in my presence. Peter assured Blount and me that the government of Hungary would be most cooperative with the Vatican but that there were some matters, such as the appointment of certain church personalities, where Hungarians would have to prevail. The foreign minister, having been told by the ambassador that this was not a concern of the United States government, agreed that the cardinal's continued stay in Budapest was not desirable and that his death in the embassy would not benefit anyone.

Incidentally, the visit of the postmaster general provided an interesting insight into the thinking of the cardinal. Mr. Blount had asked me to introduce him to the famous refugee in the American embassy. I had warned him that the conversation might be difficult, but I was prepared to take him into the cardinal's office. After the introductions, the cardinal told his visitor that anyone who came to Hungary and spent any money here was helping to extirpate Christendom. After this stiff rebuff, which left the postmaster general somewhat at sea, the cardinal told him, without further ado, the story of a little Hungarian parish priest who reportedly had been killed by a communist. The communist was sentenced for the crime by a lower court, but the decision was promptly reversed by a higher one. When the postmaster general noticed the medallion of Benjamin Franklin above the fireplace, he changed the conversation by referring to the fact that Benjamin Franklin had been the first postmaster general of the United States. Mindszenty, not fully comprehending, said yes, and added that the last good president of the United States had been Roosevelt the first! This led him into the usual tirade against Woodrow Wilson.

Monsignor Cheli met with me in the lobby of the Duna Intercontinental Hotel on the morning of September 9. He told me that the government of Hungary had complied with most of the requests of the Vatican and that he was satisfied with the arrangements for the departure of the cardinal. He said that Monsignor Zagon would arrive shortly with a letter from the Vatican, asking the cardinal to meet with the pope in Rome prior to the convening of the Synod on September 30. Cheli went so far as to suggest a special plane to take Mindszenty out of Hungary, a proposal I told him the cardinal would never accept. I was certain that the cardinal would want to leave here in his full regalia and in a manner where he could be seen by the Hungarian people. He could be persuaded to fly from Vienna to Rome but not from Budapest to Vienna.

On September 13, Monsignor Zagon began the next-to-the-last series of conferences with Cardinal Mindszenty, which would lead to his departure on September 28. Monsignor Zagon kept me informed of the general content of his conferences. It was clear that Zagon was persuasive, and it was equally clear that Mindszenty was stubborn, as he had been all of his life. Mindszenty kept raising new conditions and Zagon kept reminding him of the promise he had made to the pope. Zagon's optimism grew. Mindszenty had agreed to leave on September 27. Then on September 16, in a last session, Mindszenty told

Zagon that after a sleepless night he had come to the conclusion he could not leave by September 27.

Zagon came into my office, threw up his hands and said, "He has knocked over everything." Obviously worn out from the negotiations with the cardinal and weary of the whole affair, he said he would ask to be relieved of his mission. He said he could not continue. He felt it was a hopeless task. I suggested to him that he telephone the Vatican from my office in order to inform his chiefs regarding the turn of events. He hesitated for a moment, but then permitted me to put the call through. After a brief conversation in Italian, he was told to proceed to Vienna and get in touch with the Vatican again. I concluded that the only chance the Vatican now had lay in a renewed plea by the pope himself.

Somewhat to our amazement, Monsignor Zagon was back on September 18. He had new instructions from the Vatican. Zagon told me he was to stay until the cardinal had left the embassy.

When the cardinal received the news from Zagon on September 18 that the pope warmly but firmly asked him to come to Rome before the opening of the Holy Synod on September 30, he appeared to be ready for the news. He did not, according to Zagon, appear too surprised at this turn of events. He stressed his readiness to continue to be obedient and asked only if a delay in his departure could be arranged by one day, that is, September 28, 1971. This request, of course, was readily granted. It looked as if the end of the road was in sight. During the next ten days Cardinal Mindszenty was more active and received more visitors than he probably had in the nearly fifteen years he had spent at the embassy. He was saying his farewells to distant relatives and friends, all of whom had been contacted by the Hungarian officials and had received their permission to come into the embassy and say good-bye to the cardinal. There followed the expedition of the memoirs to Vienna, which was concluded to the satisfaction of the cardinal a day or two before his actual departure.

Monsignor Zagon became a jack-of-all-trades during this time, arriving at the embassy with new, empty suitcases, helping the cardinal with his packing, and staying with him during moments when he undoubtedly dreaded the approach of September 28. It was noticeable, however, that the cardinal's spirits improved, once the decision was final.

I took the cardinal's memoirs out myself, placed them in the trunk of my car, and delivered them for safekeeping to the American embassy in Vienna, with strict orders to release them only to the cardinal himself or his designated representative.

Cardinal Mindszenty celebrated his last mass on Sunday, September 26, with the faithful contingent of Catholic officers as well as a sprinkling of non-Catholics. He announced at that time his imminent departure. There was scarcely a Hungarian employee who did not know about his impending departure, but not a word appeared in the press. In fact, not a word of his departure leaked during the entire period, either in Budapest, Rome, Washington, or Vienna. On September 27, a Monday, he asked to make a formal call on me. He was correct and formal and somewhat stiff in his demeanor. He thanked the American government, the American people, and me for the hospitality that had been granted him during the past fifteen years. He expressed his appreciation for the care that we had shown in dealing with his memoirs. I wished him well for the future, which led him to say that it was unimportant what happened to him as an individual, but it was his native land that concerned him. This in turn led him to the same topic with which our meetings had begun in 1969: the loss of two-thirds of Hungary's territories as a result of the Treaty of Trianon. I asked him if he would agree to pose for snapshots, which he readily did. Clem Scerback took the pictures.

September 28 was a beautiful fall day in Budapest. Nearly everyone was in the embassy long before it opened for business. The cardinal celebrated his last mass, attended by three of his congregation. A little before 8:00 A.M. he presented me with a copy of a book put out by the Vatican and UNESCO containing reproductions of Raphael's paintings in the Vatican. He also asked me to distribute to the members of the staff medallions and rosaries that had been brought to Budapest by the papal nuncio in Vienna, Archbishop Rossi.

The plan for his departure, which had been carefully worked out by the Vatican representatives with the Hungarian authorities, called for his leaving the embassy at 8:30 in the morning. He was to go with the papal nuncio from Vienna and Monsignor Zagon in the nuncio's car. Monsignor Cheli would drive a second car. The government of Hungary was furnishing motorized escorts fore and aft with a doctor in the rear vehicle.

At 8:15 A.M. I called for him and Archbishop Rossi. My staff had been asked to line up in the corridor outside his quarters so that the cardinal could say good-bye to them. I thought the process would take at least ten minutes, but had not counted on the fact that he would depart as cardinal, blessing the crowd, rather than shaking hands with each individual member of the embassy staff. Thus it was that we arrived downstairs in the lobby a few minutes before the cars had actually arrived at the entrance. I asked him and Archbishop Rossi to join me at one of the small tables in the lobby. The cardinal launched into a discussion with the nuncio in Latin, but apologized to me quickly for using a language which I presumably did not understand. I told him that all I remembered of Latin was *amo, amas, amat, amamus, amatis, amant.* Within minutes Zagon appeared to say the cars were in front.

At 8:28 A.M. I led the cardinal across the threshold of the embassy, whereupon he ceased to be in asylum in the American embassy. He climbed into the papal nuncio's car, realized he was not in the place of honor, and quickly went over to the place of honor. We said our farewells and the cars were off. His departure was watched by all members of my staff from windows high up in the building. There were no Hungarians in the vast square. Indeed, all streets leading into the square had apparently been blocked off. The departure of the cardinal was, however, recorded by a policeman on his camera in the little guardhouse in front of the embassy. The recipient was *Paris Match,* a Parisian magazine in the style of *LIFE.* the photo shows the cardinal making the sign of the cross and me pointing to the car, which was interpreted by some wicked minds as "Get out!"

Thus Cardinal Mindszenty left the United States embassy in Budapest on September 28, 1971, which he had entered on November 4, 1956, nearly fifteen years before. At 11:23 word was flashed to me by prearrangement from Vienna that the cardinal had crossed the Austro-Hungarian border. The cardinal was now outside Hungary. It was not until a few minutes before 3:00 in the afternoon that the world learned of his arrival in Rome. Thus came to an end one of the most bizarre events of the twentieth century—the asylum of a cardinal of the Roman Catholic Church in an American embassy.

The departure of the cardinal from our embassy removed the last and most important stumbling block to improving our relations with Hungary. Secretary of State William P. Rogers came to Budapest on July 6, 1972, the first secretary of state to visit that capital since World War II, perhaps ever. He and his charming wife were hospitably received by the Hungarians. The secretary took time out from his round of calls to sign a consular convention, giving greater protection to our citizens traveling in Hungary. We met with Janos Kadar, the chairman of the Hungarian Communist party since 1956. I had been the first western ambassador to be received by him some months earlier, since in communist countries at that time the rule was that party officials not in the government had no business dealings with western, capitalist ambassadors.

I accompanied the secretary to the meeting with Kadar. There were only two Americans in the room and four Hungarians, including Kadar and the foreign minister, Janos Peter. In a wide-ranging dialogue that lasted two hours, Kadar paid tribute to the American ambassador, saying that he had worked hard and successfully to normalize U.S.-Hungarian relations. He added that the ambassador had pushed us very hard toward that goal, which led Secretary Rogers to reply, "Yes, he pushed us pretty hard, too." At the same time, Kadar pointed out realistically, that while we wanted to be friends, we could, of course, never be allies. He spoke of his efforts to improve the lives of the Hungarian people, a task at which he has been phenomenally successful. Hungary enjoys a better living standard and greater freedom of expression than the other communist bloc countries, while at the same time remaining securely in the communist empire. This may change of course in the near future.

The secretary, undoubtedly unintentionally gave his ambassador the biggest boost any chief of mission could get, by addressing me by my nickname, "Al," and frequently seeking confirmation from me of his replies to Kadar. This was not lost on our Hungarian hosts.

At a luncheon on the terrace of our residence, the secretary proposed a gracious toast to our Hungarian guests—some fifty of the highest officials of the Hungarian government and party. His genial and warm personality evoked an equally warm response.

Visitors now came in droves to Budapest. Elizabeth Taylor, together with her husband at the time, Richard Burton, celebrated her fortieth birthday at the new Intercontinental Hotel in Budapest. As her guest of honor, I enjoyed meeting her retinue, which included Princess Grace of Monaco, Stephen Spender, Ringo Starr, and Raquel Welch. The Hungarian press headed the bash, "Nothing Stops Tears Like a Big Diamond," a reference to the huge heart-shaped diamond pendant that Burton gave his wife. I found Princess Grace and Stephen Spender to be the most interesting of Liz's guests.

We had a delightful visit with Ann Landers (she was still married at the time) and her sister, "Dear Abby." My young son claimed he had a most rewarding conversation with Ms. Landers.

There was a time during the summer when everything was dormant. Our Hungarian friends went to Lake Balaton. We visited Greece and the Scandinavian countries. We never lost our penchant for travel. The commanding officer of the Sixth Fleet invited us to pay a visit to his command. His officers showed us the USS *Forrestal* from top to bottom. This huge aircraft carrier stood twenty-five stories high and had a crew of five thousand.

I had the dubious pleasure of taking off from the flight deck in a fighter plane.

Brezhnev came to Budapest on a state visit in November 1972. Much was made by the press of a chat I had with him at the airport, and other diplomats strained to hear what was said. Actually the Soviet leader asked me in Russian how I was. I replied in Russian, "fine."

A word here about the receptions, cocktails parties, and dinners an ambassador has to attend. Much has been written about these affairs, and congressmen have fumed over our embassies spending money on whiskey.

I found many of these receptions useful. Frequently they were the only occasions at which one could meet Hungarian government and party officials whom one could not see otherwise. I made it my business to spend most of my time with them rather than with diplomats of other countries, who usually could not contribute much to my understanding of Hungary. In fact, I invariably made it a point upon joining a reception to shake hands with the host, making sure that he knew I had come to his party, and then surveying the room to see who was there. Taking a glass of orange or tomato juice, I walked fairly rapidly through the throng, exchanging a word here and there, stopping to talk with an important Hungarian official, and then made my way to a back door and to my waiting car. My son Fred, observing this, called it the "ambassador's shuffle." Many years later I learned that the French ambassador to Washington, Henri Bonnet, had used this tactic to get himself out of boring parties!

Nineteen seventy-three was to be our last year in Budapest. We had been there three-and-a-half years at the beginning of the new year. President Nixon had been reelected by an overwhelming majority for a second term.

I had no expectations of remaining much longer at my post, already I had stayed much longer than my predecessors. Nor had I made any future plans, even though my sixtieth birthday in March of 1973 would, in all probability, mean mandatory retirement. Somehow I was so immersed in my job and the many activities that I was engaged in that I gave little thought to the future.

Then came the letter from the foreign service, asking me to tender my resignation as U.S. ambassador upon the start of Nixon's second term. This is customary. Every chief of mission offers his resignation when a new president or a second term begins, in order to give the president a free hand in appointing his chiefs of diplomatic missions. Nonetheless, it came as a shock. I, of course, offered my resignation and asked when I should leave Budapest. I was told to stay on until my successor, an officer on the staff of the secretary of state with much experience in the United Nations but none in Europe, and with no previous overseas experience, arrived.

By July he still had not come, and I decided to leave after our last—the fifth—fourth of July party of our four years in Hungary. Nearly two thousand people came to our garden party, and for the first time in five years, it rained, causing one Hungarian official to say that even the angels weep when the Puhans leave.

We left Budapest three days later.

# Jeanne F. Lamar

IT was a great joy to have a fine, loyal staff at Embassy Budapest. From my deputy to the lowest-ranking marine, the staff worked as a team, keenly aware of the objectives I hoped to attain. The very best was my secretary, Jeanne Frances Lamar.

Born in Missouri, the attractive daughter of a small-town lawyer, the bearer of a famous Southern name, Jeanne, upon completion of her schooling, struck out to work in a bank in San Francisco. When the opportunity came to take the exams for the foreign service, she decided to "see the world." And she did see much of the world, having served on four continents in nine American embassies and consulates. Before she came to Budapest, Jeanne had worked for four ambassadors and one consul general. Her reputation as a catalyst in embassies in so-called hardship posts preceded her. She worked tirelessly in making embassy personnel feel better in a hostile environment.

However, she was not my first choice. When the secretary I had brought with me to Budapest fell ill and had to return home, I was offered two names, and the assumption was that I knew both of the young ladies. As it turned out, I knew the first and chose her. Jeanne had left Bangkok a month before I arrived there and I had not met her. My first choice decided to return to the U.S. rather than continue in the foreign service. So Jeanne came to Budapest in March of 1970, a day before I left for consultations in Washington. Poor Jeanne had been told by the Office of Personnel that she had to report at once to Budapest, and had barely sufficient time to buy a winter wardrobe in Rome. She had only her summer clothes from Mogadiscio, Somalia.

When I returned to Budapest, she was well established in her job. Hers was not the easiest one. She was my secretary, but the cardinal, who had been in the embassy much longer than any ambassador or minister was another matter altogether. Indeed, he once remarked to a colleague upon looking at the photographs of all post-World War II chiefs of mission to Hungary that he had outlasted them all. The Cardinal took a great interest in all members of my staff and all Catholic members of the staff were expected to become his parishioners. Jeanne, as the ambassador's secretary, was a particular target of the cardinal's interest in seeking to learn what I was up to. Miss Lamar displayed great tact and diplomacy in not offending him without letting him know of my negotiations and other actions. I was struck by her intense loyalty to me—she knew instinctively when she could safely turn away an officer who simply wanted to chat with the boss and when she should let him in.

Budapest, as most Iron-Curtain country posts, was quite confining for single people. Dating with Hungarians was out of the question. Single men in the American and other friendly embassies were few in number. Under such circumstances it was imperative that much of the entertaining had to be done by people like Jeanne. All the officers, including the ambassador, always tried to include the single people in functions given by them. This was not always a favor to the singles. Many a time Jeanne had to break an engagement to fill in at the ambassador's dinner, when a wife of one of the invited guests called in her regrets.

In a small embassy such as ours in Hungary, the staff consisted of twenty-five souls. The ambassador's secretary acted as protocol officer. In diplomatic circles where protocol—who sits where, who sits above the salt and below it, who speaks English and who does not, and if not what other languages is spoken—is still important, and Jeanne Lamar excelled in this undertaking. She never made a mistake in making out the guest lists and where they sat at the table. Her relations with the Hungarian protocol people were excellent, which is a great help in a country where it was not always easy to get Hungarian officials, bank directors, opera conductors, artists, lawyers, and writers to come to the American ambassador's home, especially at the beginning of my tour of duty, when relations were still chilly between us and the Hungarians. Not the least important of her many functions was her liaison with the Hungarian locals, and Hungarian citizens working in nonclassified areas. Hers was the job of keeping my Hungarian chauffeur alerted as to when the ambassador wanted to leave—where to, what evening engagements, et cetera.

Normally, a tour of duty for a secretary in a post like Budapest was two years. At my request she stayed on until I left in July 1973. At that point she asked for a post near the U.S., since the health of her aged mother was frail and Jeanne wanted to be close to her. She was assigned to Monterrey, Mexico, where she was to go after a stint in Spanish language school at the Foreign Service Institute.

221

When we parted, I felt deeply indebted to her for all she had done to make my mission a success. But I hardly thought that a few years later she would become my wife.

# Ex-Ambassador

I learned very quickly upon our return to Washington that an ex-ambassador was about as passé as yesterday's newspaper. In the few weeks I spent in the State Department before my retirement became official, I was "debriefed" in a sort of cursory manner. The assistant secretary for European Affairs presented me with a Superior Service Award. After that a thirty-one year career in foreign affairs was over. I have no regrets and I do have many pleasant memories.

I went home and threw all my energy into refurbishing the house we had bought in McLean, Virginia, in 1965. It had been rented while we were abroad and needed a good deal of attention. It did seem strange not to have to set the alarm clock and go to the office, but as long as there was work to be done, I didn't mind. But in not too long a time, the house, greenhouse, and lawn were in the shape we wanted them to be in. I renewed my contacts with my sisters in Philadelphia and my brother in St. Louis, contacts broken during assignments overseas. In retirement I became acquainted with my grandchildren.

I now began a search for a new career, much later than most of my colleagues had done. Friends called my attention to various possibilities that might suit such talents and experience I had. When I followed up their suggestions I learned that it was difficult, indeed impossible, for large business concerns to determine what to do with an ex-ambassador. Everyone I talked to was interested but could not find a place for such a person.

A telephone call to a New York agency that scheduled speakers for various organizations and occasions resulted in their saying to me, "Sorry, there simply is no interest in foreign affairs. Now if you could find a colleague who would debate with you, we might find something." Period!

A call on a former colleague now highly placed in the German Marshal Plan—a kind of German Marshal Plan in reverse—resulted in a suggestion that I come up with a proposal that the people in charge of the Marshal Plan would look at.

This was the time when a number of states were sending their own "ambassadors" abroad to promote sales of products produced by them and to get foreign concerns to invest in our states. On a trip to Missouri, I came across an ad inviting qualified candidates to apply for such an "ambassadorship." When I appeared in Jefferson City, everyone there thought I was just the ticket to go to Germany and promote the "Show Me" state there. My last interview took place in St. Louis, where the chairman of the board of a large company had been asked by the governor to size me up. The interview was most pleasant. The chairman began by saying he could not possibly question my qualifications—I was certainly the best candidate so far. However, he had just two questions. The first was whether I could summon up the zeal I had displayed during my foreign service career. I answered candidly that I probably could not since I was older now, but that after all I was not expected to run footraces. As I understood the job, it was to make contacts in Germany that would be useful to the State of Missouri, and that I could certainly do. His second question was prefaced with a statement that in my career I had always had a staff—how would I do with just one secretary? Again, I answered honestly, and said, probably not as well, but by using my knowledge of the German language and the contacts I had made during my career, I would overcome some of these difficulties. The chairman said my answers were precisely what he had expected and that he was satisfied. In the meantime, the administration in Jefferson City changed and I heard no more about the job.

As my frustration and impatience grew, my marriage suffered and finally crumbled. The children were all married now and on their own. My wife and I had few harsh words, but all efforts to effect a reconciliation failed. We separated in 1975. I realized how difficult this was for my wife, who had, throughout our marriage, leaned on me completely. Although a woman of great courage and determination, she was unable to cope with a marriage that had failed. It was not easy for me to leave her after many years of wedlock and I did indeed feel extremely sorry. However, I felt I could no longer go on. We divorced in 1977. My greatest strength came from the attitude my three children displayed. Although they loved their mother, they told me they understood and supported me. Indeed, the bond between them and me grew stronger than it had been before my marriage ended.

Two events took place at this time that put me back on track. The first was a telephone call from a man I had met in Budapest, an American of Hungarian extraction. He had formed his own company to sell U.S. agricultural know-how to countries where agriculture was an important industry. Since his background was East European he had turned first to the country of his birth, Hungary. With his advice and help, he played a not unimportant role in turning Hungary from a corn-importing to a corn-exporting country.

The man was a genius in many respects. He asked me to work as a consultant to his Chicago-based firm on an as-needed basis. What he hoped I could do for him was to gain him an entry into foreign ministries, but also to officialdom in Washington, D.C., especially the Departments of Agriculture and Commerce and the U.S. Chamber of Commerce.

I worked three or four years with him, made three or four trips a year to Eastern Europe, and introduced him to some influential people in Washington. He paid me well, but more importantly, he gave me something to do. I realized early on that while this man had some positively brilliant ideas, his lack of interest in details and his rather high living standards would probably do him in. Some large agro-business concerns were interested in him, but he feared that he would be swallowed up by them and preferred to go it alone. Eventually this cost him his company, even his health, and finally, his life. While it lasted, however, my status as consultant gave me an insight into the problems American businessmen faced in dealing with foreign countries.

At the same time I received an invitation from Princeton University to become a visiting fellow. The Princeton program was an interesting one. It consisted of sending qualified speakers from all walks of life to small colleges unable to pay large fees to speakers for one week at a time.

I visited some fifteen small colleges from St. Olaf College in Minnesota to Talledega in Alabama, from Wheaton in Massachusetts to College of the Pacific in the

West over a period of three years. This turned out to be the most exhilarating experience since my days in Budapest.

The format was quite simple. The speaker arrived on a Sunday, was met by his "control officer" and taken to a reception tendered by the president of the college, or a dean, or a professor. I took over classes in political science, spoke of East-West relations, detente, Germany, Vietnam, a career in government, and other subjects. The students were most attentive and eager to pose questions. My work did not end when the classes were over. In the evening I "rapped" with students in their dormitories or fraternity-sorority houses. Invariably I ended the week with a hoarse throat! It was worth it. I obtained a marvelous insight into how the post-Vietnam generation of students were thinking. I also noticed the poor quality of teaching in some of the schools I visited. My remuneration was small—a thousand dollars stipend per week plus travel expenses. The college visited supplied board and room.

In 1977 Jeanne Lamar was back in Washington. We had corresponded while she was in Monterrey, Mexico, and had even met on a number of occasions. We got married when my divorce became final. There followed some of the happiest years of my life. Jeanne continued to work in the Department of State until 1981. Up to the date of her retirement, I was the head chef of our small establishment in Bethesda, Md. I had always had an interest in cooking and good food. Now I had the opportunity to practice "haute cuisine."

As my wife's retirement date came, we cast about for a retirement home. We looked in San Diego, Phoenix, Arizona, and the sun coast of Florida. As the result of a friendship formed on the golf links of Bethesda, Maryland, we were invited to visit Sarasota, Florida. Our friends showed us some eighty places to live. Sarasota, we learned, had everything we wanted—sunshine, a mild climate, good theater, opera, golf, and most important, friendly people with whom it was easy to make friends.

We moved to Sarasota in the late summer of 1981.